The Someday Solution

*HOW TO GO FROM UNSURE TO
UNSTOPPABLE
"ONE DAY AT A TIME"*

BOBBY KOUNTZ

*40 Day Writer LLC
Dallas, Texas*

THE SOMEDAY SOLUTION

Copyright @ 2020 by Bobby Kountz

Manufactured in USA

To learn more about Bobby, please visit:

www.somedaysolution.com and www.bobbykountz.com

Produced exclusively for Sum Total Coaching by:

40 Day Writer LLC

8150 N Stemmons Frwy Ste G-1094

Dallas, TX 75247

United States

www.writeyourbook.today

Design by Brandy Miller

Cover by Nathaniel Dasco

Archival images from author's personal collection

ISBN (Electronic Edition): 978-1-948672-17-7

ISBN (Paperback Edition): 978-1-948672-18-4

ISBN (Hardback Edition): 978-1-948672-30-6

ISBN (Audiobook Edition): 978-1-948672-31-3

10 9 8 7 6 5 4 3 2 1

In memory of Felix Buehler

For Miles

*"A father's love is
forever imprinted on
his child's heart."
-Jennifer Williamson*

Your Life Mattered; It Really Mattered

A Letter of Gratitude

Dear Felix,

After the CHAMPS meeting last night, I stopped for a moment to chat with your wife, Shareece. What an amazing woman! She informed me of your decision to move from active treatment to palliative care. And then she really blew my mind when she said, "Felix says hello, but, more importantly, thank you, for always being there for him with the group."

You have no idea how much those words moved my heart. It was all the confirmation I needed to know that both your family and you were going to be ok... they ok in this realm without you, and you ok in the next. What you demonstrated by taking the time to make sure your wishes were known, communicated, and understood is one of the most powerful things we can do as human beings: express our gratitude.

So, with that said, let me take a moment now to express my gratitude to you for all that you've done for me.

Felix, the courage you have demonstrated over the last several years has given me the foundation to find my own. Your determination not only to survive, but to "live" while you fought your valiant fight, has given me the inspiration to do the same, to really live. I thought to myself on several occasions, he's not only fighting; he's living; and he's making a difference for his family. I thought to myself, he makes a profound difference every time he shows up to share with the group. Chemo week or not, in pain or not, feeling wiped out or not, exhausted or not, you showed up.

You taught me lessons of persistence, courage, tenacity, determination, and will. You demonstrated valiantly and courageously the will to live. You demonstrated you knew you could make a difference, simply by showing up, and you did. You also taught me lessons of love and tenderness when you softly placed your hand on Miles's head one night after the meeting, looked down at him and said, "I love you." You gave him a hug, you walked out the door together, and I saw father and son in a beautiful moment... together. Yes, I know it probably looked like I was busy writing my hours on my volunteer sheet, but I was watching.

Felix, I know you heard me say many times to the group, I can't tell you what I would do if I were the one in your shoes, but, because of the gift each of you have given me, at least, I have a place to start. And now, once again, as you approach the final chapter of your life, you have given me the greatest gift of all... your gratitude.

I commit, this day, to never forget you. How could I? I will carry your gratitude with me each and every day of my life, in my heart and in my interactions with others. I will remember you always, forever.

Felix, you embraced my challenge early on and decided to make sure you always got "from the day" instead of just trying to get "through the day." What a gift you gave, living each day to its fullest, squeezing every drop from every opportunity to be a dad, husband, son, brother, and friend. To you, my friend, I will be forever grateful. I am a better man, father, brother, son, and husband to my loving wife for having had the opportunity and pleasure of knowing you.

And so, in closing, thank YOU!

I celebrate YOU, your life, and the invaluable lessons YOU taught me.

YOU lived; YOU loved; YOU mattered!

YOU are a champion, my friend!

Here is the quote I read to the group last night at the close of the meeting:

"The meaning of life is to find your gift; the purpose of life is to give it away."-Pablo Picasso

Written with love and gratitude this 15th day of January 2016,

Bobby Kountz, Facilitator

CHAMPS - Men's Cancer Support Group

***

Anonymity is a foundational principal of almost every support group. This letter was published with the exclusive permission of the family in the hopes that sharing it might actually inspire hope or help to ease the suffering of anyone touched by cancer.

Permission to use all other names mentioned in this book was given by the brave men and women who inspired me to commit to my very first ride...

Table of Contents

"Until one is committed, there is hesitancy, the chance to draw back, always ineffectiveness. Concerning all acts of initiative (and creation), there is one elementary truth, the ignorance of which kills countless ideas and splendid plans: that the moment one definitely commits oneself, then Providence moves too. All sorts of things occur to help one that would never otherwise have occurred. A whole stream of events issues from the decision, raising in one's favour all manner of unforeseen incidents and meetings and material assistance, which no man could have dreamt would have come his way. I have learned a deep respect for one of Goethe's couplets:
Whatever you can do, or dream you can, begin it.
Boldness has genius, power, and magic in it!"
— William Hutchison Murray

Foreword

"What do you think? You think it's going to rain?"

It was a question Bobby and his fellow cyclists were asking during our pre-ride dinner. With help from a couple of colleagues, we cultivated an impressive team of cyclists in Sturbridge, Massachusetts, for the 35th Pan-Mass Challenge (PMC). It's a two-day bike ride to raise money for cancer research and support.

Our team was a motley crew of newbie cyclists. What they lacked in experience, they made up for in hope and enthusiasm. The weather radar was clear. We were going to get drenched, but I didn't want to admit that and add to the anxiety. I could tell that a few members were regretting their decision to sign up.

That wasn't unusual because riding 192 miles in ideal conditions is tough enough for experienced cyclists; doing it in the rain, well, let's say I felt their nerves.

So, I lied. I shared, "Nah, it looks good. At PMC, it's all downhill with a tailwind. It's going to be great!"

The next morning, right after the National Anthem, Mother Nature made her statement and delivered the coldest and wettest PMC in history. It was brutal. I've been an avid cyclist since high school, and it was some of the hardest conditions I had ever faced.

It would be cliché to say I don't know how Bobby and his teammates did it, but I do. It started months before, when they committed to doing something bigger than themselves. They all finished without any mishaps. It was indeed a great day.

In The Someday Solution - How to Go from Unsure to Unstoppable - "One Day at a Time" Bobby shares his cycling transformation and how he became a PMC finisher in a matter of months. His framework will help you accomplish "bigger than you can imagine" challenges and change the world one life and one day at a time.

Through my friendship with Bobby, I know he doesn't just preach the principles in The Someday Solution; he lives them. It's helped him complete five additional PMC rides, support cancer patients across the country, achieve elite professional awards, and write his first book.

Books come into our world when we're ready to receive them, and this is true about The Someday Solution. Today we're facing a daunting to-do list. It's easy to dream of an ideal future or freeze because of the enormity of it all, but dreaming without action or by avoiding things has never accomplished anything.

Bobby's story will inspire you to take action. It's the perfect mixture of motivation, vulnerability, and courage to help you see something bigger than yourself and take action one pedal stroke at a time. So, if you're ready to be unstoppable, it's time to commit. From here, Bobby will help you figure it out "One Day at a Time."

-Michael O'Brien, President and Founder

Resilience Expert, Executive Coach, TEDx Speaker, and Author of Shift

Peloton Executive Coaching

Author's Note

During the early days of my sobriety, I was reunited with my biological mother and sister. I grew up not knowing either of them. I grew up without my biological father as well. I was raised by loving, caring, well-intentioned grandparents, who raised me the best way they knew how. I am still grateful.

My reunion with my mother and sister came at a time when I needed all the support I could get. It turned out to be a monumental pivotal point in my life. My turning point was punctuated by our reunion and a subsequent experience afforded me by my mother.

Her life had been dramatically changed by a gentleman named Jim Rohn. I remember getting a letter with a ticket to a seminar and a note that said, "Mr. Rohn helped me become who I am by exposing me to some ideas I had never heard. After I attended my first seminar, I was never the same. It's my sincere hope you have a similar experience. Be sure to take a notebook. I love you. Mom"

This letter meant way more to me than the ticket and, to this day, I'm still not sure which one was more valuable because each of them served me in a different way.

I went to that seminar. I even showed up early. I wasn't typically ever early to anything. (Did I mention my mom told me to be sure I was on time?)

Anyway, I was in my mind, just a guy fresh out of the Army, coming off of a failed first semester, who had gone back to college on the money he earned by trading almost five years of his life in the service of his country (which really meant I went into the Army to get some discipline because I had none and my grandpa dad thought it might be my saving grace, and he was right).

Needless to say, I felt like a fish out of water, or maybe even more appropriately, I felt like a fish trying to climb a tree. Einstein purportedly said: "Everybody is a genius. But if you judge a fish by its ability to climb a tree, it will live its whole life believing it is stupid." (As it turns out, like so many great quotes, Einstein didn't say it, but it's still a great quote.)

As I watched the meeting room fill up with what were very obviously some incredibly successful people, I found myself feeling more and more out of place. It appeared almost everyone in the room had brought a journal to take notes in and I felt even more foolish as I looked at my raggedy spiral bound college notebook.

I remember feeling like I didn't belong. I remember feeling small and inadequate. I contemplated leaving and then I thought about my mom and envisioned her disappointment and found the shred of courage I needed to stay.

When the silver-haired gentleman spoke, I found myself absolutely captivated by his ease, confidence, and the simplicity of his words. I was transfixed as he described how he was a simple farm boy from Idaho who had fortunately found his way to Beverly Hills after meeting a man who had changed his life.

Within minutes, I realized my life was about to change, too. By the end of that seminar I had filled an entire notebook, and the ticket my mom had given me included a personalized copy of Mr. Rohn's newly released book. It's copy 251 of 2500, and the inscription from Mr. Rohn says: Bobby, for the best of life and treasure.

I took that message seriously and I still have my spiral bound notebook from February 21, 1991. My life changed that day. I was introduced to the power of personal growth and I have tried to grow just a little bit every day, "one day at a time."

The source of my inspiration comes from my own personal journey...

COMMITS... (A Sobering Poem)

Choose to begin if you want to win. Choose to say, I choose today to begin.

Optimize all available resources. Offer help, support, and new life courses.

Manage expectations. Minute by minute, day by day, manage life now, not someday.

Make mistakes and friends along the way. The journey is simple day by day...

Inspire others and seek inspiration. After all, we're just an inspirational nation.

Together we accomplish more. Together we can avoid a life on the floor.

Success is accomplished with action. Sobriety begins with minimal traction.

Choose to live life clean and sober. Or soon you will find life is over.

Optimize every chance to learn. Commit, decide, stand tall, be stern.

Manage your life "one day at a time." Hour by hour, time is sublime.

Make your commitment; make it today. Tomorrow is never the sobriety way.

Inspire your friends and your family too. They will gladly support the brand new you.

Together we can achieve what we can't do alone. Make the call, pick up the phone.

Success comes to those who commit to their path. Commit now, no more wrath...

Choose new habits; choose new ways. Soon you will see bright sunny days.

Optimize the twelve steps and traditions. Avoid the lonely road to perdition.

Manage each step, one step at a time. No hurry, no rush, no race against time.

Make this day the day that you say, "I choose sobriety, just for today."

Inspire another to join in the cause. Simply remind them today is a pause.

Together we see what we never saw: life in all its splendor and awe.

Success has arrived at the crossroads today. Failure is always just one drink away...

Choose to believe it's possible for you. Faith will certainly move mountains too.

Optimize this new life you've been given. Begin right now to again begin living.

Manage your day or it will manage you. Drink not today or for sure you'll be through.

Make today the day that you say, "Thanks to my higher power, I am sober today."

Inspire others with your sobriety story. Share your message and your glory.

Together a journey is one we can travel. Alone what's found is the sound of the gavel.

Success smiles on those who work their plan. Success arrives today for woman or man.

Introduction

Two quotes have guided me through the arduous process of telling my story and writing this book. The first is the quote that represents the struggle and the second is the quote that represents the hope.

"When I write, I feel like an armless, legless man with a crayon in his mouth."
-Kurt Vonnegut
"When writing the story of your life, don't let anyone else hold the pen."
-Harley Davidson

The Journey

"Here" was the couch where the journey began and where I found myself, both out of shape and overweight. Over "there" was the finish line of the Pan-Mass Challenge, or the PMC, as it's lovingly known by all who participate in this incredible annual event.

The challenge was to get from the couch where I was comfortably seated in Las Vegas to the finish line at the end of the two-day, 192-mile bicycle ride across Massachusetts to complete the PMC.

I was not a cyclist. I hadn't ridden a bike in at least 10 years. Not only was I not a cyclist, I didn't even own a bike. I hadn't thought about riding 1.92 miles, let alone 192 miles, over two days. Frankly, I had no idea how I was ever going to get into "good enough" shape to complete the ride either. To say I was "unsure" would be an absolute understatement of the obvious.

The Purpose of This Book

Although this book was written about my experience, about my journey of figuring out how to go from sitting on a couch to completing a 192-mile bike ride over two days, the book is not about me.

It's about YOU!

This book is about you and your untapped or yet-to-be-unlocked potential. Hidden within each of us is everything we might ever need to do almost anything we can think of doing. This book is about helping you unlock that potential.

It's about the potential that resides inside all of us, the magic we can only ever access when we give ourselves permission. The purpose of this book is to show you how to access the highest part of yourself and to give yourself permission to become all that you're truly capable of becoming, whatever that may be.

We can only ever individually define what success means to us. The best definition of success I ever heard came from Earl Nightingale who said, "Success is the progressive realization of a worthy idea or goal." If we do anything with intention and purpose, we are already successful.

We are the ones who define what that looks like. It's not our mother, not our father, not our friends, not our family, not the expectations of society, not the expectations of our race, nor those of our creed, color, or heritage. As human beings connected to the highest part of ourselves, connected to the infinite nature of the universe, we decide individually and we come to our conclusion in a moment's notice.

"The moment one definitely commits oneself, then Providence moves too."
-William Hutchinson Murray

We empower ourselves the moment we decide. We empower ourselves the moment we commit, not sometime in the future, not SOMEDAY, but now.

The title of this book is The Someday Solution, and it's all about what happens when we become willing to "commit" now, in the moment, and without having it all figured out. The mistake most of us make is in believing that we have to have everything figured out. We don't have to have it all figured out. As a matter of fact, it's impossible to know what we don't yet know.

I had no idea how I was going to go from the couch to finding a bike, to getting a bike, to training, to learning all that I needed to learn to be able to actually ride 192 miles over a weekend to complete the Pan-Mass Challenge. I could have easily said, "You know, this probably isn't the best time for me to be doing something like this right now, but it sounds like something I'd really like to do… 'someday.'"

I was beyond "unsure." I had no idea how I was going to raise the funds I had committed to raising, but it all happened; it all developed over time. It all developed with the process that I'm about to share with you in the pages and chapters of this book, because here's what happens when you commit: When you commit, you give yourself a chance at success.

It's my intention, as the author of this book, to give you as many resources as you need to embark on your journey. The COMMITS pathway to progress that I discovered while preparing for the Pan-Mass Challenge is simple and easy to follow. There is a certain responsibility that comes along with writing a transformational book. Our words have the potential to either lift up or strike down the spirit of another human being.

I'm not a traditional writer. I am hopeful that, as a reader, you will appreciate the style I bring to my work. Almost all of my writing is what I would consider "inspired writing." I have a process I utilize to get in touch with what I refer to as my higher self. This involves the use of a variety of both meditative and inspirational music as well as the process of meditation itself along with the extensive use of powerfully inspiring and informative quotes. All of my writing begins with the inspiration wrapped up in the hidden message of a quotation.

How the Book Is Structured

There are seven chapters. Each chapter represents a letter from the word "COMMITS." The S at the end of the word commit represents "success."

The first letter of commit, "C," is "choose to begin." This is so incredibly important to understand. If you don't at least choose to begin, you'll never even have a chance to find out.

Once you do commit, it's probably going to be in your best interest to embrace "O," or a one-day-at-a-time attitude. I discovered on my journey through life that "one day at a time" is the best approach to optimize all your available resources, or opportunities.

It would also be very helpful if you figure out how to "M," manage your expectations. I'm not here to tell you to have realistic expectations. That would have ended my journey right from the beginning. Going 192 miles on a bicycle, when you don't even own one, is a pretty unrealistic expectation for most people. But if you manage your expectations, you can figure out how to break them down day by day.

To succeed, it will be very helpful for you to "M" make mistakes... and friends too. If you commit to making mistakes, and friends along the way, I assure you the journey will be much more memorable.

Make a conscious decision that you will "I" inspire others by sharing your story, and seek inspiration from those who are willing to share and from every source of inspiration you can find that will support you on your journey.

It's important to understand that you cannot do it alone... So many people try to do everything alone. It's impossible. I have struggled for years to do things alone. When I committed to completing the PMC, I found the power of "T," which is very simply a team. Together we accomplish more.

And of course, finally "S" is for success. "S" is the bonus chapter. "S" represents whatever you want it to be... Only you can decide what success means for you, but remember success is the natural result of commitment.

When you look at a marathon as an example, there are those who come out of the gates very quickly, and they achieve massive, massive results in such a short amount of time. And then you have those who embrace the marathon as a journey, as something to be completed, not even something to be done, but... something to be accomplished, overcome. That's not the right word; it's something to be achieved, still not the right word... What is it when someone climbs Mt. Everest? What is that called when they get to the top? What is that sense of accomplishment that they feel when they get to the top? Oh... I know; it just hit me: "conquered."

Well, that's the opportunity you get to have, with whatever challenge you choose to attempt. Using the framework I have established for you in the contents of this book, you will learn "how to go from unsure to UNSTOPPA-BLE," "one day at a time."

The Culprits

Fear and self-doubt are responsible for more death than all of the wars of the world combined because they have killed people's hopes and ambitions and left a corpse where a thriving human being once stood. The real walking dead are those who have given up on their dreams, goals, and ambitions. Their imagined self-limiting beliefs and subsequent behavior are controlling their actions.

They trudge through life going to a job they hate, doing work they hate, and barely surviving paycheck to paycheck because fear, self-doubt, faith, self-belief, and self-confidence are not active in their life in the proper proportion. How do I know this? They were completely out of proportion in my own life.

Maybe for you, one of the elements is under control, but what about the other elements? Where do you sit in the equation with the other elements? How prevalent is each of these elements in your life?

What do you fear? How much faith do you have in yourself and your ideas? How about belief? Do you believe in yourself? And finally, how is your self-confidence? Take a minute right now, and make an honest assessment. Be true to yourself. Be honest! Remember, this is just a snapshot in time, a picture of where you are right now in this moment. And, this is just for you, so you know where you stand. This is not who you are. Remember, you are not your thoughts.

The one common thread amongst all of the great teachers and philosophers throughout time is that they all said in one way, shape, or form, that it is imperative that we both know and be true to ourselves. The ancient Greek aphorism "know thyself," or "gnothi seauton," is one of the Delphic maxims inscribed in the pronaos of the temple of Apollo at Delphi. Socrates, The Tao Te Ching, The Bible, The Egyptians, and Buddha, they all said the same thing: ~Nosce te Ipsum~

OK, back to the equation: fear, self-doubt, faith, self-belief, and self-confidence... The goal here is to increase our self-confidence. When we tip the scales in favor of self-confidence, then fear, self-doubt, and self-limiting behaviors lose their stature. They lose their "perceived" power. In truth, the only power they ever had was the power we each assigned to them.

In and of themselves and by themselves, they actually hold no real value. We, each of us as individuals, assign the value. Our experiences have led us to assign value arbitrarily without any real proof other than our own or our parents', siblings', or peers' experiences influencing the value we assigned.

Self-doubt is replaced with self-confidence by simply facing our fears and doing what we fear anyway. Self-limiting behaviors are replaced with self-actualizing behaviors as we overcome obstacles and build confidence step by step, goal by goal, accomplishment by accomplishment, "one day at a time," on the road to success and achievement.

This book provides an easy seven-part process that automatically shifts the equation so that the proportion of faith, self-belief, and self-confidence increases and that of fear and self-doubt decreases, automatically tipping the scales in your favor. When you agree to implement this achievement framework, when you agree to COMMIT first, then figure it out, you will be empowered to accomplish almost anything, overcome what has up until now seemed impossible, and shift from feeling unsure to believing you are absolutely UNSTOPPABLE!

Your Invitation

This book was written first to inspire, second to tell a story, third to inform, and finally to transform limiting beliefs, misconceptions, and misunderstandings into understanding. It was written to both show and tell readers about what's possible. It was written to show not only what's possible, but more importantly, what's possible for anyone who reads and applies the lessons that lie waiting inside this book.

"The mind, once stretched by a new idea, never returns to its original dimensions."
-Ralph Waldo Emerson

Once you read this book, you will find yourself seeing things differently; you will have an erectness to your carriage and a skip to your step. You will have a quiet confidence about you that you can't quite explain, but yet somehow know is the truth. What you will discover is your truth. The smile that everyone else notices on your face will be the result of realizing what you already knew but had not yet internalized.

Come along with me. Join me on the journey. It's a ride you'll never forget, I assure you. Come on, join my peloton, just as I joined the peloton of OB, Nancy, Lara, and all of my friends. Join us as we ride together to make a difference in the lives of those who are battling cancer. Join me on my journey...

Better yet, invite me to join you on yours. This book is not about me. It's about you, so let's shift. What's your journey? What is it that you really want to do, be, or become, that you've never given yourself permission to do, be, or become? Decide right now that it's possible for you, and together we can achieve it, one day at a time.

We can only ever know what the next step is, and by embracing the step we're taking, that step will give rise to the next step, and the next, and the next. And before you know it, you'll find yourself at the finish line, like I did after two days of an incredible adventure, which showed me something about myself that I didn't even know existed... You too can learn how to go from unsure to UNSTOPPABLE!

By tapping into the collective conscience of the universe and your fellow man, woman, or child, you will become UNSTOPPABLE! When you make a "commitment" grounded by a strong "why," free from any concern of "how," that commitment becomes possible. The commitment to the outcome, the desired result, or stated objective is our only concern. When the "why" is big enough, the "how" will always present itself. If the "how" does not present itself, it simply means the "why" wasn't big enough.

"How" is not our concern. The cursed details of "how" have killed more dreams and crushed more ideas than any other event in history. The ideas were crushed and killed before they ever had a chance to develop, because the need to know the "how" killed the idea and the dream while it was still just a fledgling thought, before it was ever acted upon.

Before we begin, I want you to let your imagination wander. I want you to take a moment and think about something you have always wanted to do, but, for whatever reason, you have yet to take on the challenge. Maybe like me, you contemplated writing a book for as many years as I did before I finally took my own advice and decided to simply COMMIT to the process.

By beginning with the end in mind, I knew I could write the type of book that could be a game-changer for the person ready to explore all that was possible for them if they would simply begin.

So, let's take the journey together. Not mine, but yours. Let me be with you on the way. Know that you can reach out to me, through my words, through the words that are in this book at any time you feel yourself struggling. Know that I'm just one word away, one page away.

Chapter One: Choose To Begin

It All Began With A Text Message

"All things are created twice, first mentally, then physically."
-Stephen Covey

"Hey Bobby, Lara and I were talking, and we think you would be PERFECT to join us this year for the PMC. It's a great event and a lot of fun. Whaddya think?"

My reply was brief. I was intrigued. I had no idea what the PMC was.

"Hey Nancy! Cool... What kind of event is it?"

Nancy's reply came swiftly, "Oh, it's a bike-ride fundraiser for the Dana Farber Cancer Institute..."

I thought to myself, a bike-ride fundraiser? What makes me a perfect candidate for a bike-ride fundraiser? I'm 52 years old and hardly in shape. But I wanted to help if I could, so I replied back.

"Interesting, tell me more."

Nancy's answer was vague. "Well, we're putting together a conference call to discuss all the details. I'll send you an invite, OK?"

I innocently agreed to the call. "Sure..."

The conference call was the hook. My "yes" was the sound of the hook being swallowed. All that remained now was for Nancy and Lara to slowly reel me in. Yes, I was a fish...

During the conference call, I learned I was being invited to participate in a 192-mile, 2-day event.

"It's a blast!" I was reassured.

"You're perfect for it!" I was told.

Somewhere during the call, I was introduced to the PMC Motto: "Commit... You'll figure it out!"

This is what they say to everyone to keep them from running as fast as they can in the opposite direction.

A conversation slowly unfolded in my mind:

The voice of responsibility spoke first, This is a huge commitment. I'm already overwhelmed with commitments. How on earth am I going to find the time to add this one to my already overcrowded schedule?

My internal relationship monitor spoke up next, How will my wife feel about me spending yet even more time away from her? She's physically incapable of riding a bike, so asking her to join me isn't a possibility. She's already somewhat resentful of the amount of time I spend on the road, away from home, away from her. Will this drive an even deeper wedge between us?

Fear found its voice, I'm afraid! What will happen if I fail? Even worse, what will happen if I succeed and those stories that I've been telling myself all these years that I'm not good enough are suddenly challenged? Who will I be without my stories?

Yet underneath the fear and the creeping anxiety over how my family would receive this news was a "still small voice" that spoke to me in a whisper. Ever so quietly I faintly heard the words: You could find a way to do this. What are you afraid of?

And then another voice, much louder than the first, broke through the chaos. This voice was excited and busy painting pictures in my head of me, smiling on that bike, crossing that finish line after having ridden those 192 long miles, triumphant, UNSTOPPABLE! How would you feel if you actually did this?

I envisioned the possibility to do what I felt I was born to do – to help others – dancing in front of my eyes. I saw not just the cancer patients that I would be helping with the money I raised, but the people who may have been held back, just as I had been, by those stories born of pain and rejection, suddenly seeing in my story a hope for a better tomorrow, a chance that maybe those I hoped to serve would be capable of being and doing more than they believed they were capable of being and doing.

And with the vision came the anticipation of a future that was as yet unseen but would be revealed by the decision to say YES!

My mind now began to race as I tried to figure all of this out. How would I do it? Isn't it interesting the way our minds almost automatically jump to "how"? I didn't even know where to begin. I moved between fear and anxiety followed by excitement and anticipation. I thought, I can't do this. But – what if I can? What if all that's standing between me and the vision of that future where I am finally doing the work I know I was born to do is my "yes" to this moment?

Concerns and Challenges

My protest began right after that call. I took my time crafting a text response to Lara that went something like this:

"Lara, today's call was really interesting. There are just a few problems I think we should discuss... You remember my initial concerns, right? No bike, no clue, no nothing..."

Lara replied back. "Can you talk NOW?"

I hesitated. It would be easy to put her off. But I told her the truth. "YES."

My phone rang. It was Lara. Imagine a Jamaican-Bostonian accent. It was her idea of having fun with my quandary. In her best Jamaican impression, she said, "No worries, Mon. Everyting work its way out just fine, Mon. We do everyting the PMC way. Just commit... You'll figure it out."

What I wanted were specifics, details, logistics.

What I got was, "Bobbay, everyting just have a way of coming togetter once you commit! Trust me, it's not as difficult as it seems. Let me tell you about how I got my bike."

And she did. That wasn't enough.

The questions kept coming to me, "What about...? What about...? What about...?"

Finally, she stopped me and asked a question."Bobby, do you trust me?"

There was silence between us. I didn't know how to answer this.

"Bobby, are you there? Hello, Hello?"

I begrudgingly spoke, "Yes, Lara, I'm here and I trust you."

Her answer put me on the spot, "Then commit! Right now, this minute with me, on the phone, repeat after me 'we can do this together.' Right now, repeat after me.'"

When I didn't repeat the words, she spoke again, this time firmly, "No, really, right now, repeat after me."

In that exact moment, everything changed for me. I truly understood that I wouldn't be completing this journey alone and that with the PMC motto, and the help and support of a team, I started to believe I could, that we could and would together, not only succeed, but we would do it with style and flair.

The Magic of Commitment

I learned that day, once you commit, even with reservation, the collective forces of the entire universe line up to support your commitment. All you must do is "choose to begin."

Here's what unfolded next. I was an oncology nurse by background, and I had facilitated cancer support groups for years. I was at my multiple myeloma group at the Caring Place, where I volunteered, and I shared with the group my bold plans as well as my many concerns about all of my "issues."

I am a bit embarrassed to say it, but I was actually kind of whining... mainly that I didn't even have a bike.

As soon as I was done whining, a hand shot up. I was almost annoyed but said, "What's up, Ron?"

Ron, a two-time cancer survivor, had a huge grin on his face and said he had a road bike I could ride. He even offered me a helmet, gloves, and some other things, too.

You see, before being diagnosed, Ron was a huge cycle enthusiast and had to literally park his hobby in the garage with not just one but three other bikes. I had just experienced the first bit of "magic" from the PMC motto. It was truly in that exact moment I knew I was destined to make this journey. I literally saw it as a divine sign, complete with all of the hairs standing up on my arms and my neck.

Next, there was a doctor who told me where to go and who to see so I could learn about cycling. That was when I met Terry from the bike shop. I told him about my commitment to complete the challenge and I watched the color drain from his face before he asked, "When is the event?"

When I told him it was five months away, there was a huge sigh of relief. We began an amazing conversation.

He said, "Let's get you completely familiar with riding and then we can discuss what gear you need and might want. I recommend you get used to riding before you pick out your shoes and clip-ins, you know, pedals."

I said, "Sure, whatever you think is best..." I literally knew nothing about cycling.

He began giving me instructions. "Just start by riding around your neighborhood and the general area. Then you can come and do a group ride with us. I will teach you some basics."

I said, "Cool." I wouldn't see Terry again until our Sunday ride.

Training began. I started in my neighborhood, as Terry suggested. I became familiar with the bike, shifting gears up and down to match the terrain and my desire to go faster or slower, or to be able to pedal more easily going up a hill. I ventured out of the neighborhood but stayed in the general area. I didn't want to get too far from the house and my comfort zone. By day three of training, I felt I was ready for my first "real" ride.

I mapped out the distance to the "M" Hotel from my house. It was a ten-mile round trip, a major milestone to be sure. I made my way there with no real concerns as it was downhill leaving the neighborhood and the wind was at my back on the way.

The ride back was a little different for two reasons: first, the wind was now in my face and blowing about 20 miles an hour, and second, the hill I had come down on the way out was much steeper than I realized upon my return. In the easiest gear possible, I pedaled as hard as I could to get up the hill heading home. It wasn't pretty, but I made it!

I repeated that ride a couple of times as it seemed like a great way for me to build up my confidence. I knew I had already done it once, so I believed I could certainly do it again. I felt like I was making real progress.

Sunday morning was my first ride with Terry from the bike shop. We met at 7:00 and off we went. The goal of the group ride was to go at a pace everyone could maintain and for all of us to finish together. I remember Terry riding alongside me and coaching me through the gears. He constantly reminded me to get off my butt and pedal while raised up off the seat. I was beginning to learn the importance of resources.

About halfway through the ride, Terry stopped and adjusted my seat because it was too low. That small adjustment made an amazing difference. I was learning.

When we finished the ride, we discussed my first immediate needs. I left the shop that day with a small pouch to go under my seat which held 2 spare inner tubes, a small tool kit, and the tire tools. I also purchased a front and rear light for the bike so I could ride at night or before dawn if need be.

You Will Never Have It All Figured Out

Where people get stuck is wanting to have everything revealed to them before they begin. But that can't happen. You can't see the next step until you take that first one.

Everything started happening when I said, "Yes!" Once you commit and start taking action, you will figure it out.

I now have two voices in my head. The first is that still, small voice that says to me, Commit. Everything will be provided to you in ways you can't even imagine. The second is the voice of the PMC motto, Commit... You'll figure it out.

The idea of commitment came up again and again as I began to write this book. At first, my thought was Who am I to write a book? And that still small voice told me, Who are you not to write a book? Don't you have a story? And can't your story help someone else? And I knew the still small voice was right.

Whenever we begin any kind of a new project, explore a new idea, or take on some kind of a new challenge, we have a very limited frame of reference from where to begin. Understanding this as not a challenge, but an opportunity instead, gives us the permission we need to become curious, the same way children are curious about almost anything they don't understand. Curiosity is a superpower!

You Are More Than Enough

Whenever we make a decision to do something, the actual decision is usually only made after careful consideration and much, oftentimes way too much, deliberation. More great ideas have died in this stage than probably all the great ideas that have been acted upon combined. When we engage our mind in thought about a new activity, particularly something we have never done before, we have absolutely no frame of reference as to whether the idea has any merit or if we are even capable of going through with it.

What stops most of us before we ever get started is some version of an I'm not enough idea that sneaks into our mind before we even realize it's there. The typical thought is I'm not good enough, smart enough, athletic enough, etc. If we want to move forward and not be trapped by our potential for negative thinking, we are best served to simply make a choice to just begin the process.

Baby Steps

We don't have to know anything about "how" we intend to actually do what we are considering. We must, however, choose to begin. And it's best to just begin from wherever we are with whatever we have. Once again, the decision to begin is the most important piece of the puzzle. Just commit! Choose to begin.

Each and every journey begins with the first step. Then we just put one foot in front of the other and take the next step, and that step leads to the next, and so on. Oftentimes, the next step can't even be seen or imagined until we take the first step.

We only need to take a small step; even just a baby step will do. And if we get stuck, then what? If we simply pause and reflect for just a moment, we can almost always see the next step. What exactly constitutes a small step? A small step can be defined as almost any activity that moves us in the direction of our desired outcome, stated goal, or intention. Yes, choosing to begin is a great example of a small step.

Focus On The Why

What we don't have to know is the how. In fact, it would be best to ignore and avoid any and all concerns about the how. What we need to focus on is our why. I recommend becoming absolutely crystal clear about the why, about your why. When the why is big enough, the how will show up, eventually.

When I decided to write this book, I didn't know how to do it. What I knew, what I was sure of, was why I wanted to do it. I was healthy and able to do something about cancer patients, so I wanted to do something to help them, to motivate them, to share with them that everything they do matters. So I started writing my ideas one page at a time. The how presented itself little by little as I wrote.

Many cancer patients let their diagnosis define them. I thought if they saw me do something I've never done before, they would be motivated to do what they want. I hoped they wouldn't let their limitations get in the way of their dreams. There is a lot cancer patients can do, a lot they want to do, a lot for which they have a why. And yet, they let the lack of how get in the way. Now I say to them, "If I can write a book, you can do whatever you dream."

> *"Don't let what you can't do stop you from doing what you can do."*
> *- John Wooden*

All you have to do is commit. Take that first step. If you choose to begin, the next step will appear. Starting is a choice.

"Choices are the hinges of destiny." –Pythagoras

Everything we are and everything we will ever be will be determined by the choices we either do or don't make. We can either choose to begin or not. We can choose to learn more or not. We can choose to study or not. Our destiny is not some predetermined outcome which has been decided for us. Our destiny is what we make it, and our choices are what determine it.

As human beings, we have the greatest gift available to us on the planet. We have the ability to think and reason; we have free will. There is no other creature on earth with this amazing gift. Each and every day we receive an allotment of time to accomplish all that we choose to do in any given 24-hour period. Obviously, we cannot do everything in one day, so we must develop effective strategies to manage our choices for each day. If we leave this important decision to chance, the day will surely run us, instead of us running the day.

Decide right now, in this moment, not tomorrow, not "someday," but right now. Decide what it is you really want and decide what you are willing to give in return for its attainment. This one decision will have more to do with your destiny than anything else.

When we decide to take full responsibility for our choices, we are empowered, in that moment, to make as many mistakes as required for us to succeed and achieve. It is only the unsure mind, the apprehensive mind, that second guesses and questions each decision with what-if questions.

Our destiny hinges not on the decisions of our past, but on the decisions we make today, and the decisions we will make tomorrow, and the next day, and the one after that. And that is because all of the decisions we make are only ever made "one day at a time." Let the past serve as a reflection for the future. Destiny is a choice.

The teachings of Pythagoras give us a foundation from which to begin any new endeavor we choose. The ability to think and reason is viewed by many as a curse instead of a gift. When we pause to reflect, however, no matter what our view, we must, at a minimum, acknowledge what the ability to think and reason allows us. All other creatures in the animal kingdom operate purely from instinct. They are governed by a preconceived set of conditions that keep them from making any choices independent of instinct. The same is not true for human beings. We can, at any point in time, tear up the script of our lives and begin again with new information.

"I am always doing what I can't do yet, in order to learn how to do it."
-Vincent Van Gogh

Van Gogh didn't say I am always "thinking about doing" what I can't do yet. No, he clearly stated "I am always doing." When we "do" what we can't do yet, we learn the how.

In other words, just like Edison, Van Gogh realized the only way to learn how not to do something was to do it. Once we finally succeed, once we finally learn, then we can say we did it.

Ideas and theories are great because they give us direction. The "scientific method" serves a very valuable purpose. It provides a framework for how to begin. It doesn't give us an answer, however; only the experiment does that. And, although we first think about the experiment, nothing really happens until we begin.

So then, what does it actually take to move forward on an idea? Understanding that all things are created twice, first in thought then in action, provides a simple two-step process to begin. First, decide what you want by thinking about the desired outcome or destination. Second, act on the thought or idea by choosing to begin. COMMIT!

When faced with taking on a challenge or attempting something we have never done before, one of the most difficult struggles we face is simply where to begin. It is difficult to get started if we don't know where to start. This was the exact dilemma I faced when trying to figure out how to write and publish this book.

One way to start is to simply commit to begin. It is in the "act of commitment" that a decision is made to actually "do" something. By beginning with the end in mind, we can take a series of logical steps to work through almost any challenge and accomplish almost anything we once thought impossible, step by step, one day at a time.

The process begins the moment we commit. Once we commit, we"choose" to begin. This is the first part of the COMMITS process. My own experience of preparing for and successfully completing the Pan-Mass Challenge when I had no knowledge of cycling or how to even begin preparing for this type of event provides a solid example of how working through the steps to solve challenges both created and identified solutions I didn't even know existed.

I learned we don't need to know all of the steps in the process. All that's required is a willingness to just take the very first step in the process and each next step will reveal itself as we move forward.

> *"Every human mind is a great slumbering power until awakened by a keen desire and by definite resolution to do."*
> *-Edgar F. Roberts*

What great ability lies just below the surface in your life awaiting the opportunity to emerge? What keen desire has been sitting on the back burner of your life waiting for the right moment to be expressed? What action step could you take today, instead of someday, to awaken the sleeping giant within you? What is it that if you just gave yourself permission and applied a little bit of consistent effort everyday, you could materialize for yourself?

Human beings have the ability, with sound thinking and planning, to accomplish almost anything. And yet every day, thousands upon thousands of individuals resign themselves to "lead lives of quiet desperation," as Thoreau so eloquently captured.

We must be willing to take on the most difficult of journeys, which is to go inside our own mind and find out what is waiting there for us. We must resolve to take on the most difficult battle of our life. We must win the battle with self. Our first and best victory, as Plato stated, is to conquer self.

"The secret of making something work in your lives is, first of all, the deep desire to make it work, then the faith and belief that it can work, then to hold that clear definite vision in your consciousness and see it working out step by step, without one thought of doubt or disbelief."
-Eileen Caddy

We must believe that our efforts can and will bear fruit. We must learn to believe in our own capabilities to execute the action steps that will bring our vision to life. Our doubt and disbelief must be uprooted and discarded the same as we would discard any behavior that no longer serves our best interest.

"If I have the belief that I can do it, I shall surely acquire the capacity to do it even if I may not have it at the beginning."
-Mahatma Gandhi

The word "if" may be one of the most remarkable words not only in the English language, but in every language. "If" sets the stage, if you will, for whatever comes after it. "If" sets the tone for all that is either possible or impossible. Everything that comes after the word "if" is dependent on how the word has been structured in both our language and our thinking.

All that comes after the word "if" is predicated on how the word is used and in what combination. "If I have the belief that I can...." is contrasted with "even if I may not have it." It is what we "believe" that establishes the foundation for all that is possible. Without belief, there is nothing.

"Once we believe in ourselves, we can risk curiosity, wonder, spontaneous delight, or any experience that reveals the human spirit."
-E.E. Cummings

With any new endeavor or even a simple idea, the first step starts with the choice to begin. It begins when we commit to pursuing the idea and deciding we are willing to do the work to bring the idea to life. It is critically important to understand that we don't have to know how, but we must know why. The strength of our why determines our courage, our resolution, and our sacrifice.

Once we commit, we take step after step and develop our confidence as we move forward in the process. Our confidence grows as we face and conquer each and every obstacle that arises while working to bring the idea to life. We become more and more comfortable trying new approaches; we begin to embrace our curiosity; wonder returns to us like when we were children; and we begin to be less calculating and more spontaneous.

Before we know it, we are alive with enthusiasm, confidence, and belief. And the end result of this awakening of our human spirit is an experience of bliss, often referred to as joy.

"Whatever you do, you need courage. Whatever course you decide upon, there is always someone to tell you that you are wrong. There are always difficulties arising that tempt you to believe your critics are right.

To map out a course of action and follow it to an end requires some of the same courage that a soldier needs. Peace has its victories, but it takes brave men and women to win them."
-Ralph Waldo Emerson

The decisions that matter are the ones we make on purpose, the ones we have conceived as possible for us and our families. If it were not possible, we could not conceive it. The moment we were able to conceive the idea, it became possible. Our idea became a possibility the moment it was born.

What does it take to bring an idea to life? Resolve, commitment, determination, persistence, belief, tenacity, and a course of action. What does it take to stand in the face of fear and move forward anyway? It takes both belief and courage. Courageously believing in the decisions we make and refusing to quit when others suggest we should are what defines the difference between a commitment and a wish. Commit.

"You too, can determine what you want. You can decide on your major objectives, targets, aims, and destination."

-W. Clement Stone

Each of us is gifted with the ability to determine what we believe at the time to be our best course of action. The reason I say we are "gifted" is because we are not like the animals that must follow their instinctual drive... No, our gift is the ability to both think and reason. However, when we are operating from habit, we have a tendency to either take our gift for granted or forget it altogether.

To achieve different results, we must be engaged in different thinking. We must decide what it is that we really want. It is impossible to reach a destination if we don't know what the destination is. We need to know where we are and where we want to be. Only then can we find a way to bridge the gap between the two points.

Most of us don't aim too high and miss. No, the majority of us aim too low and hit. We need only look to the books of history to understand that mankind is capable of remarkable things. When we set our sights high, when we determine with purpose and clarity our desired destination, there is nothing that can keep us from our desired objective except ourselves.

Decision is the mechanism of action that both sets our course and makes the minor adjustments required to keep us on track over time. Once we decide that we will succeed no matter what obstacles may present themselves, then it seems we are on a direct path whether it be around, over, or through, to our desired outcome, as long as we refuse to quit. Persist and win!

"Decide what you want. Believe you can have it. Believe you deserve it and believe it's possible for you." -Jack Canfield

If anyone ever had a reason to quit, if anyone ever felt they had tried hard enough, if anyone ever believed that maybe they had done their best and it just wasn't meant for them, it would be Jack Canfield.

How many rejections do you think Jack Canfield and his partner Mark Victor Hansen had to overcome before all the work they had poured into Chicken

Soup for the Soul would finally pay off? How many sleepless nights? How many disappointments? How many failed presentations? How many no's before the magic word yes was finally heard?

"Chicken Soup for the Soul" was rejected by 144 publishers. If we had given up after 100 publishers, I likely would not be where I am now. I encourage you to reject rejection. If someone says no, just say NEXT!"
-Jack Canfield

Chicken Soup for the Soul has sold over 123 million copies just in North America alone and over 500 million worldwide!

When we decide what we want, when we believe we can have it, and when we believe we deserve it, we have established our belief in what's possible for us. When we decide, we are saying to ourselves that we will persist no matter what. When we decide, we commit. When we commit, we win, eventually. The combination of patience, belief, persistence, and the ability to decide is unstoppable!

The combination is unstoppable if we are willing to try and do things we have never done before, if we are willing to consider there may be another way, if we are willing to examine our habits and see if there is room for improvement.

"A habit is a lifestyle to be lived, not a finish line to be crossed. Make small, sustainable changes you can stick with."
-James Clear

As a general rule, we tend to develop habits and rituals, both of which are crucial. Because life can become so demanding, we have a tendency to follow patterns that emerge over time. Initially, our habits may actually serve us well. But, they typically only change if we focus on changing them. If we are striving to achieve or accomplish something we have never done before, we will most likely have to develop some new skills, methods, and habits to achieve the results we desire. This one decision, choosing to begin, becomes the catalyst for change.

First, we must believe that change is possible for us. Second, we must decide what it is we want and then be willing to do whatever is required to achieve our desired outcome. Third, we must decide what the next best step is in the process. Before we realize it, we have both done what we needed to do and achieved what we previously had not.

"I know of no more encouraging fact than the unquestionable ability of man to elevate his life by conscious endeavor."
-Henry David Thoreau

Conscious endeavor involves choosing work or another pursuit that matters, not for someone else's satisfaction, but one's own. It is deciding on a course of action or path of fulfillment and satisfaction.

When we live our lives on purpose with passion and conviction doing exactly what we choose with purpose and clarity, then we are engaged in a conscious endeavor. For some, this type of work involves finding a way to express creative capacity; for some, it may be becoming the very best mother or father possible; others may choose to lead with passion and inspire as many as possible to become the very best they are capable of by supporting their growth and desire to achieve.

Whatever the endeavor may be, as long as it is a conscious choice, the opportunity to elevate one's life will exist. Choose to live with passion and purpose, commit to making a real difference in the service of others, and you will find yourself living an elevated life.

In order to live an elevated life, we have to be willing to climb. We have to be willing to embrace adversity, difficulty, and challenge with the understanding that these elements are simply presenting themselves so that we might be better prepared for the struggle.

"Whatever the struggle, continue the climb. It may be only one step to the summit."
-Diane Westlake

When we both qualify and quantify something, we give ourselves the very best chance of making a real commitment. Once we empower ourselves through the act of making a decision, or a commitment, we then, in that exact moment, also prepare ourselves mentally that "whatever the struggle," we will continue, we will strive forward, we will search, we will find, and we will make it to the summit, step by step.

Life is full of many different types of stories. One of the stories I remember my mentor Jim Rohn discussing was about a female executive he met at one of his corporate presentations. She was actually the CEO. He described her as articulate, wealthy, powerful, and sophisticated. Mr. Rohn was always learning, so he simply asked her, "How did you get here?"

She said, one day, I asked my husband for $10. He looked at me and said, "What for?" She said she decided right then she would never, ever have to ask again. She then said, "I began my journey. I started reading. I started learning. I made a commitment to "myself" that I would do whatever it took, no matter how long it took, so I would never have to ask again. And I haven't."

Behind every story that grabs our attention and captivates our curiosity, there is struggle. In most of the stories, or speeches, or plays, or operas, or books, someone wins. What we see on the stage or in the book, we don't often get to see in real life. Most of us don't get to see the struggle, and yet it is there. We don't get to see the climb, and yet it is there. And if the summit is shrouded in clouds, we don't get to see the climber reach the summit either, and yet they did.

Victory is often a silent celebration experienced only after we are willing to continue the climb, whatever the struggle. To others, the summit looks unattainable, because when they look up, all they can see are the obstacles between them and the summit. The committed climber looks to the summit for directional guidance but only focuses on the very next step that moves them toward their goal. Remember, sometimes the summit is shrouded in clouds; it might be just one step away.

Victory will only ever be an option if we first "choose to begin..." Before we can ever reach the crest of the summit, finish the race or the ride, learn a new skill, start a new business, write our first book, give our first speech, or do anything else we haven't done before, we must first "choose to begin."

Chapter Two: One Day at a Time

Day by Day

Time has been described as our most valuable resource. Everything happens within the confines of time, and it happens "one day at a time."

If you're attempting something you've never done before, once you've decided to do it, the next step appears in front of you. Sometimes different steps appear in front of you. Choosing the right next step can be challenging. You will need to use all the resources available to you to get as much information as you can to choose that next step. So you want to optimize all your resources, but how do you know what the available resources are? You don't, not all at once, anyway. You can't know what you don't know. You'll learn about them and figure things out as you go, day by day.

When I chose to commit to the Pan-Mass Challenge, I suddenly found myself about to take on this epic thing that I'd never done. I asked myself, "How will I ever figure out what I need?" This wasn't the first time I had asked this question.

Nearly thirty years earlier, as I stood at the crossroads, I asked myself, How will I ever do this? I had never even considered what a life without alcohol might look like. It had become such an integral part of my life. When I drank, everything in life that I found troubling and difficult melted away, as I melted into a space where whatever was going on, whatever I was feeling, and whatever was happening didn't really matter anymore, at least not while I was inebriated, anyway. However, when I awoke in a stupor the next day, all of my problems and all of my challenges were still there, only now they were even more pressing, so I simply drank more.

Eventually there came a day when I realized I was either going to end up in prison or dead, and neither option was appealing to me when I wasn't smashed. Finally, I even considered what my life would be like without me in it. After a little more consideration, I realized what I really needed was some help.

With the support, help, and guidance of my sister Linda, we created a plan that would leverage every single resource available. Had it not been for my sister and her husband's willingness to take a risk on me by inviting me into their home, I don't believe I would have made it. I would have been just another statistic, a number, an early headstone. I am so grateful!

Climbing Your Everest

Life is full of challenges. Sobriety was just one of the many challenges I faced. In our lifetime, each of us will have difficulties and obstacles to overcome. They will test us. They will challenge us to grow. They will force us to change, which is exactly what we need, yet we often resist it.

Some of the challenges will be insignificant; others will be small; some will be large; some will be monumental. For me, the challenge of sobriety was both monumental and looming like a great mountain in the distant skyline.

Mountains are conquered step by step, one small step at a time. Fear is an insidious monster. It turns what should be a rational easy decision into a complex quagmire of doubt. Combine self-doubt with a lack of self-esteem and a poor self-concept and you have a recipe for disaster. I experienced each of these self-deficiencies, and beneath it all was resentment, feelings of abandonment, and, worst of all, feeling unlovable.

Everyone has a different mountain. Only you know what yours is. Overcoming my addiction was mine. Abstinence might be your mountain, or tobacco, or food, or education. These mountains may seem impossible to climb at first, but once that first step is taken, the climb continues, and once the summit is reached, we realize what we created in our mind was much bigger than the mountain, and the climb was not impossible as we had initially believed.

What we believe affects our choices. If we just have faith in whatever our higher power is, whether we call it God or Universe or whatever, we will be able to commit and know in our hearts that the how will present itself at the right time.

My saving grace was when I finally made my decision to give up alcohol. I asked God to take away the desire, and he did. I also asked that the craving for tobacco be taken away as well, and it was. Had it not been for the grace of God, I don't believe you would be reading this book. As a matter of fact, I don't believe I would have been here to write it. I am so grateful. In asking for God's grace, I made a commitment that if He would guide me out of despair, I would work diligently the rest of my life to make up for my transgressions.

I have.

This book has been part of my pathway, and it wasn't until the editing process of my manuscript that I gained the courage to finally tell my story. Over the years, I have helped many friends find the courage to face their fears, and I have managed to help a few people fight their inner demons of doubt, despair, drugs, and alcohol, but I have fallen short of writing about and sharing my own personal story of recovery.

This book has been one of my mountains. In fact, it has been my highest and steepest one, my Everest. It's the one thing I have allowed to hold me back for years because of my fear of telling this story and the shame that accompanies it.

"The cave you fear to enter holds the treasure you seek."

-Joseph Campbell

Fear will keep you from achieving your full potential. It will keep you from looking in the cave. It kept this book languishing on a hard drive for years, while I mustered the courage to share the words you're now reading.

We All Have a Story

There is a certain catharsis that comes from writing that no other form of therapy can accomplish. It's the reason almost every recovery program encourages journaling. When we get the thoughts out of our head and onto the page, we can slowly begin to make sense of them, one day at a time. They don't always make sense, at least not at first, but, eventually, with persistence and patience, we begin to make sense of them.

This is how it worked for me. It's different for everybody. When we're attached to the story we've been telling ourselves our whole life, it isn't so easy to let that story go. We can think of our story with the same affection we have for a favorite piece of clothing. I know some men who have cried when they found out their well-meaning wife or mother threw away their favorite T-shirt. If it's not an article of clothing for you, maybe it's your favorite pair of shoes, your soft, comfortable shoes, whose heels are completely worn and whose soles are so thin that every pebble you step on feels like a giant rock, yet you resist parting with them.

For many of us, our stories have served us so long we can't imagine our life without them. It is, as a matter of fact, the most common thing that keeps many an alcoholic trapped in the vicious cycle of addiction. Alcohol has for so many become such a central part of their lives they can't see themselves not drinking. They don't see themselves fitting in socially without a beer or glass of wine in their hand. It was a bit different for me because whether at 15 or 28, I don't ever remember drinking responsibly, or, as people call it, socially. I first used alcohol to fit in with a group of kids who looked at me as the outsider from the other trailer park, the one where the adults lived. Alcohol bridged that gap, and it bridged it quickly.

Southern Comfort was my first experience, and its smooth sweet taste was easy going down, and as I took each shot I was given, I was applauded and cheered on. I was "accepted."

Shortly after that first experience I was stealing booze from my Dad's bar and taking it to the park where I mixed it with coke to take away the bite of the whisky I pilfered from my father. I knew it was wrong, but the risk was worth it because when I showed up with the booze, I was accepted.

Not long after the drinking began, probably within weeks, it was decided we should all leave the trailer park to go to the city park to "party." I wasn't supposed to leave the trailer park, but what was I to do? I didn't dare take the risk of being called "chicken" or worse yet a "p*ssy," so I went. So did my sister, my adopted sister, Linda.

We never saw the cops because they walked up in the dark unannounced until they were right on top of us. The mag-light shining in my face seemed brighter than the sun, and I still remember the shocked look on the face of the young cop who incredulously asked me how old I was. I didn't look a day over twelve. When I told him I was fifteen, he asked "Do your parents know where you are?" I said no.

The ride in the back of the police car was long and lonely. As we pulled up in front of our trailer, I came to my senses and was sure my heart was going to pound right out of my chest. The look of astonishment on my father's face was seared into my memory forever. Then the look shifted to utter disappointment, and I think if he weren't a stoic man, he would have cried. I knew I had broken his heart; the damage was done. I knew real guilt for the first time. It had come from a look and tears that never materialized because the disappointment quickly turned to rage.

My dad should have hit me, but he didn't. The trauma from having already lost a son not to death but to his own uncontrolled anger kept him from repeating the same mistake. Had he simply given me the whipping I deserved, I would have gotten over it. His silence and refusal to look at me was far worse than any corporal punishment he could have dispensed. Instead, I was left to suffer silently in my guilt and shame, and it was into this place I would recede for the next ten years of my life.

My grandparents never found out Linda was at the park with me. She didn't get caught. She never got in any trouble, and I never told.

I wasn't trusted with a car, so instead I was forced to ride a motorcycle. My grandpa dad didn't believe I could cause any serious damage on a motorcycle, so that's how my driving began as riding instead. In the meantime, my adopted sister had the coolest little mini-truck complete with personalized license plates that read SUGAR.

Her with her little truck and me being stuck with my motorcycle just made me feel all the more insecure, just a little more unlovable. After all, she was the "real" daughter and I was her brother who wasn't even worthy of formal adoption. In fairness to my grandparents, it should be understood they saw no reason to formally adopt me. I had the same last name, they called me "Son," and that was good enough for them. I don't ever remember being asked how I felt about it. They clearly didn't know.

After the initial incident in the park, I shut down emotionally and internalized every failure, mistake, and misstep I made and never bothered to try to explain what I was feeling. My own biological father was right there in Vegas, and yet I didn't fit into his family so I wasn't a part of it and lived instead with my grandparents. I remember wondering, what kind of father wouldn't want his own son? I internalized that too.

No More Presents

My mom had been out of the picture since I was a little boy, and, for years, I held out hope that one day she would show up and take me away. It never happened.

I remember when I was much younger my first Christmas without a present from my mom. As I pulled all the presents from under the tree and passed them out, I remember continuing to look and search, thinking I had somehow missed a present, and when I looked into my grandma's eyes, I knew there would be no present from my mom. I asked why, and she simply said she didn't know. Obviously, it was a conversation she was ill prepared to have, or perhaps she would have saved me from the anguish of looking for a present she knew wasn't there. I internalized that experience too. I was six.

The real kicker came a couple years later when a jealous friend trying to inflict pain said to me, "What's wrong with you? Why don't you live with your dad? He comes around, but you don't live with him, so he must not care about you." I internalized that too.

I could go on and on with various stories, but I think by now you get the idea. I didn't understand. I was confused. I felt unlovable, and that was my reality, whether it was true or not.

Oh Canada

To make matters worse, for reasons unknown and not understood by me, my father moved as far away as he could. He went to Canada and started a new family, without me.

No father, no mother, emptiness where love should have been, but at least I had my grandparents. And it went on like that and the years passed by.

In junior high, when I was finally settled and feeling like my life was perfect, my grandparents announced we were moving to Canada. I was beyond shocked. I was pissed. I was incredulous. The fact that we would only have a limited number of things we could take with us only fueled the rage inside. I was being ripped away from my friends and I had to leave half of my stuff behind too. It sucked!

Canada was an absolute disaster. We experienced the coldest winter in forty years. Once, it was forty degrees below zero for an entire week. It was so cold our breath actually froze with every exhale! Shortly after the frozen week from hell, our school bus was rear ended by a semi, and I was ejected from the bus. I landed in a ravine, broke my leg, experienced internal injuries, and nearly died. That sucked too!

Vegas

That miserable winter and my miserable accident brought us to Las Vegas. My grandparents vowed to never be cold again, so they returned to the city they lived in during the late 50s. Vegas in the 70s was not the Vegas they remembered.

In just a little over a year's time, we had gone from the suburbs of Reno to Canada and to the trailer park where my troubled life began. I was so naïve and ill equipped for what Vegas had in store for me. This was the beginning of my descent. It was that first summer that everything changed. With no kids my age and no friends available in the adult park where my grandparents had placed me, lying about my age so they could get in, my life began to unravel.

You now have an idea of at least part of my underlying story that led me to what I found would numb the pain. Whatever pain we experience in life, we either deal with it or find a way to bury it. I chose to numb it, and what I found was when I was numb, the pain was at least tolerable.

High school had its ups and downs. I remember wanting to be on the wrestling team. That didn't work out, and the why isn't important. What is important is the high school I attended was outside my neighborhood because my grandparents, who had gone through the depression, wanted me to have a trade to fall back on in case other things didn't work out. I became a carpenter as that was the lineage I came from. My dad, my grandpa dad, his dad, and his grandpa, who had come from Holland, had all been carpenters. And so it was.

The work ethic I had learned as a paperboy served me well as a young man. When all my friends were having fun in high school, I had a job. I now had all the money I needed for all the booze I could ever want to drink. I was a functional high school drunk. I managed to both graduate and keep my job throughout high school.

I was abandoned for the second time after high school. At least that's the way it felt to me at the time. I was only seventeen, but my grandparents decided they were going to retire. They left Linda and me set up in a different trailer with the understanding she was in charge, which was the right choice because as irresponsible as I had been about almost everything, she had been the opposite. It still didn't sit well with me, and, frankly, neither did their leaving. I felt like I still needed them, and, to me, it felt like since I was done with school, they were done being my parents.

Shortly after my grandparents left, with no one to keep me grounded, I drifted further and further into my addiction. It wasn't long before my life was coming off the rails. I experienced fights, busted lips, broken teeth, evictions, and even jail. It turns out if you don't go to court for traffic tickets and you don't pay your fines, they issue failure to appear warrants and when you get caught speeding the next time, you go to jail.

You're in The Army Now

It was in jail that my salvation came. Well, at least, the road to salvation came from being in jail. My grandparents bailed me out and got me cleaned up and back in shape, or in good enough shape to get the Army to take a chance on me. With a promise of college and a four-year commitment, off I went to basic training.

I was older than most of the kids just out of high school. I quickly became a squad leader. I was sober, and I was stronger than I had been in years, but the cigarettes were killing me. They made it hard for me to do the runs required for basic training, but I got through it. My first weekend pass was nothing but trouble. Lawton, Oklahoma, is a military town just off the base of Fort Sill. Like most military towns, it's full of bars, and we tried to go to all of them. I was back on the treadmill... like a hamster on a wheel. The vicious cycle began again.

My advanced training was the beginning of my battle with the bottle, again, and the bottle was winning. My first duty station was Fort Stewart, Georgia, and with Savannah not too far away, the weekend parties began. If I could have just drunk socially, I probably would have been fine, but I never knew when to quit. I managed to avoid any serious trouble, but it was brewing.

When I got my orders for Germany, I was beyond excited. I was finally going to see the world. What I found in Germany was the best beer and wine I had ever tasted. I made some German friends too, and Germans love their beer and wine. For most people, it would have been a match made in heaven. For me, it was a match made in hell. I was drinking every day. As soon as I'd get back to the barracks after the day, I'd have a beer in my hands and a cigarette in my mouth. The weekends were all drinking fests with a beer in one hand and a bottle of Jack Daniels in the other.

Soon I found myself in an alcohol awareness class trying to make sense of why other people could drink normally, but not me. I got a second glimmer of what was driving all of this, but I wasn't ready to deal with my demons, so I tried to drown them instead.

When it was time for me to leave Germany, I was done with the military and they were done with me. Once you tell them you're not interested in reenlisting, they can't get rid of you fast enough.

Time For College

Coming back to a place you got away from by going into the military to get away from all the trouble you had been in, is not the best plan, but Vegas was where my family was, so that's where I came back to.

I found a roommate and began to use some of the money I had earned to go to college. It was a slow start at best. I began at the community college, and, to give you an idea of how far behind I was and what I had done to my brain with all the drinking, my first math class was Math 95D. The D stood for developmental. I felt good I had avoided the lowest math entry point possible, 93D.

That first semester was both a blur and a disaster. I failed more classes than I passed. However, it was also the semester I took Psychology 101 from a History of Rock & Roll professor named Ray Rich. Mr. Rich was an intriguing guy and, for whatever reason, took a liking to me. I think he looked at me as a social experiment and he was determined to get through to me. I remember him asking me several times why I was so angry and who I thought I was hurting with my reckless behavior. Yes, I went to class drunk regularly.

One day after class Mr. Rich asked me to stay behind. I don't remember all the details of what we talked about, but what I do remember was him telling me he hated seeing someone as obviously bright as me throwing his life away. I remember him asking me if I had any goals, aspirations, or dreams. I told him I wanted to become a psychologist so maybe I could somehow make sense of my life.

He said good. Start here. Then he handed me a document printed on what looked like parchment paper with words scrolled on it about how all men dream but not equally... Ray Rich saw something in me that I could not yet see in myself, and he did everything he could to get me to "wake up."

Over summer break after another mishap that led to an arrest for reckless driving, I got really depressed. My grades had come in the mail and I believe I had like 3 F's and a C. I drank myself into a stupor, blacked out, and when I woke up, I broke down crying. I sobbed and I sobbed and I sobbed. I remember feeling empty, devoid of all emotion except the despair I was feeling at having ended up right back where I started.

I was at the crossroads and I knew if I didn't get help, I was going to end up dead or in prison.

And now we are finally right back where we began in the chapter, where I told you about how Linda agreed to give me a chance...

Beginning the Climb

With the help of the VA, particularly the one-on-one counseling I received to help me deal with my feelings of anger, resentment, and abandonment, our weekly men's group, and AA in between, supported by the lessons I learned at the Grapevine Fellowship, I began to slowly feel human again, "one day at a time."

Where I live, gambling is an Everest for many who initially embrace it as fun. Don't get me wrong. Just like most people are able to drink socially and responsibly, thousands view gambling as a form of entertainment and play responsibly, stopping when their fun money is gone. Challenges arise for most of us when we lose control of our ability to remain in control and let our emotions make decisions our conscious rational brain should be making instead. People don't set out to become addicted to anything usually. It's something that happens slowly over time, one day at a time. Often, learned behaviors that can also be unlearned.

Many of the veterans in the program I attended were also in counseling for negative behaviors associated with not being able to control their urge to gamble. And what made matters worse for them was the connection between drinking, gambling, and smoking. Whatever it is you want to change about yourself, it's possible. It probably won't be easy, and it won't happen overnight, but I can assure you it will be worth it.

The battle may not be easy. "Easy" and "difficult" are words. We're the ones that assign value to words. We determine if something is easy or difficult, and the degrees of these adjectives vary from person to person and circumstance to circumstance. It's important not to compare your circumstance with someone else's.

And remember, as you make progress, in the direction of whatever change you're making, don't compare yourself to someone else. Don't compare your progress to someone else's progress. If you're going to make a comparison, make it to where you began. Everybody's mountain is different.

Individual Awareness

By the time a climber finally reaches base camp at Everest, before they ever take one step toward the looming ascent, they have climbed the mountain hundreds of times in their mind.

If the climber didn't believe what they were about to attempt was at least possible, they wouldn't even try. Changing an addictive behavior begins with awareness, with the belief that change is possible. We each climb our mountains in our own individual way. There is no one way to climb a mountain. There is no perfect way. There is the way of trial and error. There is finding a way or creating a way when it appears there is none.

"We don't see the world as it is but as we are."
-Anais Nin

Perception is everything. The way we see things determines the relationship we create with them. There was a point in my life where alcohol was the solution to my problems. Once I perceived it for what it was, it became easier to choose to stop using it.

"Today I choose" is an effective strategy. It can be a gamechanger. The statement made by the individual to the subconscious mind wakes up a part of the brain that has been asleep at the wheel. It says, "Pay attention! Listen! A command is being given." "Today I choose" is a way to regain control "one day at a time." It's a statement, a decision, a commitment.

Each of these decisions will be made in the moment, in real time. Just like for the climber preparing for the ascent on the mountain, calculations will be made and routes will be chosen, but success or failure will be decided on the mountain step by step. The same is true of the individual battling the demons of their addiction. They will create a plan with their sponsor or recovery support team and then they will go to work on the plan "one day at a time."

And if everything goes according to plan, and if the weather cooperates, and if there are no mishaps, the climber will at least have a chance of reaching the summit. The same is true for the individual battling addiction.

Before the climber ever takes the first step toward the summit, they have taken thousands of steps thousands of times, they have practiced again and again, one day at a time. It was this one particular strategy that was probably the most impactful in my own recovery.

However, I made the strategy bi-directional for maximum effect. Not only did I see myself succeeding again and again, but I tempered that image with a profoundly graphic image of failure as well. I went to an area of town many would describe in their cities as the wrong side of the tracks. This is the place where the downtrodden congregate. This is the area where the outreach shelters are and what you will often see are those not doing so well in various states of disarray. I selfishly looked for the worst of the worst. I looked for the drunk lying in the gutter, covered in their own filth and vomit. Once I found a real image that matched the one I had envisioned, instead of turning away, I stared, and I stared long enough until the image was burned into my mind where it would stay forever.

The climber burns the image of the summit into their mind. An Olympic athlete will do the same. They see themselves succeeding at the highest level before they ever do, and they put in the work to reach their own individual summits.

This cumulative, methodical, consistent, committed effort adds up overtime to become the fabric of the life of the climber, the athlete, the entrepreneur, the adventurer, or anyone who overcomes massive adversity in their life. It doesn't matter what your goal is or who you are, this applies to everyone.

We are the culmination of each of our lived experiences. If we let them, they will define us, our lives, and our future. Our beliefs, based on our life experience, have the ability to keep us stuck in base camp or support our climb toward the summit. Peaks, valleys, ups, downs, canyons, and chasms are all part of life. Our ability to navigate them intentionally is what determines our outcome. Sobriety was a mountain. Completing my first PMC was a mountain. Writing this book has been my Everest.

Just For Today

"Just for today" is a strategy for breaking down the week. The newly sober men or women are indeed climbing the mountain, but they are not ready for Everest. Often, they are not even prepared for the hill of tomorrow, so, instead, they are encouraged to focus on what's directly in front of them.

"Just for today" is a confidence builder. When I first embarked on my sobriety journey, I had zero confidence I would be successful. To say I was "unsure" is an absolute understatement of the obvious. I believed it was possible because others had done it before me, but I thought they must have somehow been different or better than me.

Sobriety is indeed a critical component of the process, but recovery is more about recovering things like dignity, decency, self-respect, self-worth, self-image, and so many other self-related elements of life.

Using "just for today" alleviates some of the overwhelming anxiety and fear. Most of us have heard the phrase by the inch it's a cinch, by the yard it's hard. Recovery is like that. By the mile, it is sure to take a while. Whatever miles are accumulated on the road to sobriety, they will be accumulated, one day at a time. This has been my experience and, all these years later, I have accumulated over 10,000 days "one day at a time."

I stopped counting a long time ago and shifted my energy instead into activities I could first gain an understanding of and then apply hours of reading and practicing toward. Somewhere along the way I came across the idea that if you made a conscious decision to apply yourself to a chosen field of endeavor, you could become an expert in that field after about 10,000 hours of application.

Although I don't claim to be a sobriety or behavior expert, I believe I have earned the distinction of being a sobriety scholar. Advanced degrees are bestowed on those who commit to their chosen field and write a thesis on a subject of interest in their field.

This book is not only my Everest; it's my thesis about what I believe is possible for a human being willing to stake their very existence on the idea of not only what's possible, but more importantly, what's possible for them with commitment, practice, determination, and persistence.

Viktor Frankl wrote about this idea in his book, Man's Search for Meaning. As a holocaust survivor, he witnessed massive tragedy and triumphed over his own. This book is just one of the many that helped me make sense of my own struggles. It helped me understand "my story" was, by comparison, not a tragedy. It helped me make sense of my struggle without discounting my experience.

Learning and curiosity have been central to my success of accumulating over 10,000 days. I optimized all my resources, one day at a time, and learned as much as I could so that I could take the best step, every step of the way.

School was good for me although it was often stressful and overwhelming. It was not the ideal situation, and it concerned my counselor from the VA, but since we talked about everything, he felt it was a risk worth taking as long as I agreed to be honest with him about the stress I experienced.

I made two friends in college for whom I will be eternally grateful. Jeff and Carmella saw something in me I had forgotten existed. It was their faith and belief in me and their support of me that helped me bridge my belief gap. They even openly encouraged me to believe in their belief in me, until I was ready to believe in myself again. I never forgot that lesson and I offer it to others regularly all these years later. I am so very grateful!

Finding Your Courage

As I have finally found the courage to share the story you just finished reading, I realize this story is a whole book in itself. After all, 10,000 days provides a lot of material to choose from. What I have shared here barely skims the surface. If my words have somehow touched you, then in my mind this book is already a success. For those of you wanting to know the rest of my sobriety story, you will have to wait for my next book.

All these years, I held on to my story and considered sharing it an impossible challenge; I thought of it as my Everest. Now that I've overcome my limiting beliefs, I feel it may turn out this book was not my actual Everest. When we aim high and miss, we still come out better off than where we started. Some even discover success beyond their wildest measure. When we aim low and hit, we usually get about what we expected or less. "One day at a time" almost anything is possible, even what seems impossible.

When you have your why, find your courage and commit. Take that first step. Once you're involved in the activity, you'll learn more about what you're doing, and your next steps will appear before you.

"Tell me and I forget. Teach me and I remember. Involve me

> ### *and I learn."*
> ### *-Benjamin Franklin*

You will reach your mountain if you commit and take it one day at a time. What you discover about yourself and what you're capable of on the journey will be way more valuable and important than the summit.

Training Was a Mountain

As I began the training process, I realized the only way I was going to get from where I was to where I wanted to be was to break the process down into more manageable pieces. Training for the PMC brought me right back to remembering how I had gotten through every challenge I had faced since that fateful day so many years earlier when I had been standing at the crossroads.

I realized that everything I had ever done had all been done the same way I had done sobriety. It had all been done, "one day at a time." I even realized things I had done before sobriety had been done day by day, one day at a time. The Army had definitely been like that. As a matter of fact, it's actually structured that way. First, they break you down, and then they build you back up so you're better, stronger, faster. As I was training for the PMC, I used every single resource available. I even used an experience from basic training to get me through a particularly difficult training ride one day... If you want all the juicy details, you're going to have to stick with me.

As I mentioned earlier, when I accepted the challenge to participate in the PMC, I didn't have a bike, and Ron offered me his bike.

The Gift of a Bike – Ron's Side of Bobby's Story

Before I got cancer, I rode my bike every day. My younger brother was a triathlon competitor and he encouraged me to get into it after he'd been doing it for about 5 years. It turns out that decision would end up helping me to survive cancer ten years later.

My battle with cancer started with prostate cancer. I was cured, and then

I got sick again and couldn't figure out what was happening. I went to a urologist thinking maybe something was wrong with my prostate again. He did an x-ray and spotted a mass on my spine.

This time, I went to the Cancer Center. That's when they confirmed the mass on my spine and told me I had multiple myeloma, a blood cancer, that was affecting my whole system. Being healthier because of all my bike riding was a huge help to me. I was past the normal age where they would normally recommend a stem cell transplant, but because of my health condition, they put me on the list anyway.

While I was at the Cancer Center getting treatments, I spotted a flyer for The Caring Place advertising a support group and thought, what do I have to lose? The description of The Caring Place was: "For Those Touched by Cancer." Well, I'd been "touched" twice, so I decided to give it a try. This was in 2013.

It was there that I met Bobby Kountz. He was one of the volunteers who helped facilitate the support group for those who were diagnosed with multiple myeloma. One night, while sharing at the group, he told us that some colleagues from his company wanted him to participate in a 192-mile bike ride. As he described to us what they wanted him to do, he seemed a bit incredulous!

There were just a few problems with their idea, Bobby admitted. First, he didn't own a bike. Second, he didn't know anything about cycling. Third, he frankly wasn't exactly in shape to go on a 192-mile bike ride. When I looked up at Bobby with a big smile on my face and my hand held high as I waited for him to call on me, I was grinning from ear to ear both inside and out. You might even say I kind of looked like the cat that ate the canary. I simply said, "I've got a bike. I've got a bike you can ride!" Bobby looked shocked.

I then offered to help him with whatever I could. I told him I had a bike that was just about brand new. I wasn't able to ride my bikes anymore because of the cancer. I tend to lose my balance a lot. It felt good to be able to pass on the joy of bike riding to someone new.

Bobby and I set an appointment time for him to come and pick up the bike. A lot of people talk about doing things and don't ever take action. I wasn't sure Bobby was going to show up. I was so glad to see him when he did. I knew it meant he'd committed to the bike ride.

I showed him the bike and then showed him how to shift the gears and work the brakes. I also showed him the equipment he would need so he would know what to look for and gave him some of mine to get started with. I told him he could use the bike as long as he needed to, and if he liked it, he could buy it from me if he still wanted it after his ride.

It was a special moment for me to know that I'd been part of helping Bobby achieve one of his first goals. It was even more special after he completed the Pan-Mass Challenge. He came back to me and paid me for the bike. He said he liked it and he wanted to keep it. I don't think Bobby rides every day like I used to, but I know he still rides regularly, and I'm glad to have been a part of that.

There's a joy in bike riding you just can't get out of anything else you do. I like to encourage people to ride. In fact, I inspired four of the guys I work with to start riding bikes. One of them just bought an upper end bike this month...

Communicate

Relationships are the first resource you have. Don't discount any relationships. After all, that's how I got my bike. It showed up in a conversation, in an instant, with the group I was supporting. Literally, in an instant, my excuse about not having a bike was gone. Now I had to show up and now I had to deliver. Isn't it intriguing how the universe works?

Resources start coming together when you start talking about what you've committed to do. You tell a couple of people in conversation what you're up to, who then put you in touch with other people who can help you, and then those people connect you to other people.

"The moment one definitely commits oneself, then Provi-

dence moves too."
-William Hutchinson Murray

Getting the bike led me to the bike shop. At the bike shop, I met Terry, the owner. I had been referred to him by one of the physicians I called on. I also met some of the kids who worked at the shop who were cyclists themselves. They all seemed very intrigued by my commitment and were eager to help. I still remember the first time I walked into the shop like it was just yesterday. I told Terry about the doctor who had sent me to see him and why I was there. I remember how the color drained out of his face as I told him about the ride I'd committed to and that I didn't know anything about cycling.

When I explained I had plenty of time to prepare, I watched the color return to his face with a smile. He then said, "You have no idea how many people have come to me over the years to tell me about their fantastic plans, and I have to be the bearer of bad news telling them they're not going to be prepared in two weeks to do what they've committed to. Even with the amount of time you have, unless you get really serious, you won't be prepared either. If you are serious, then meet me back here on Sunday and I'll take you out with a group of riders and we'll get your training started." You'd better believe I was there that next Sunday and so my training began.

You're not alone. You're only ever one piece of information away from finding the next step. After that first ride with Terry and a few more, I began to settle into a training routine of riding short rides in the morning before work, and longer rides on the weekend when I had more time. My first long ride was a failure. I had one bottle of regular water and one bottle of supplement water. I started cramping on my return ride and was still at least 10 miles from home. I'd already done 40 miles that day. I literally had to get off my bike because my legs were cramping so bad I couldn't keep going. My legs simply wouldn't function anymore. I did have enough information to know that you have to start stretching and not just sit down. You have to stretch and work your legs through the cramps as you're working through the pain. Eventually, I got through the cramps and got back on the bike and I asked myself the question, "What's the lesson here?"

I reached out to some of my new biking friends who began asking me questions. I realized that I needed to be sure that I had additional packets of supplements to put in my water so I could replenish the electrolytes I'd been losing. I didn't realize how fast I was losing the hydration and minerals my body needed. I made a commitment that from then on I would always be prepared. I needed that experience in order to make sure it never happened again. I said to myself, "Remember, when you go out for a long ride, you have to come back the same distance, and you need to be prepared for that."

Had I not prepared so extensively, had I not put in the time, effort, and energy, I never would have finished my first Pan-Mass Challenge. I relied on the memories of those cramps and my "failures" to build the motivation required to stay committed. Every failure was a learning experience in disguise.

The ant will try until it succeeds. If you put something between an ant and the anthill, whatever it is you put in front of it, it will stay at it until it figures out how to go over, under, around, or through it. It will not quit until it succeeds.

All through the summer, the ant prepares for winter. All through the winter, the ant thinks of summer. The experience that feels so hard and so difficult will pass. Winter will pass, snow will melt, and the ant will be out there all over again.

The ant philosophy, which I learned from Jim Rohn – a terrific resource – keeps me motivated anytime I want to quit. And wanting to quit is part of the human experience. We all get discouraged. We all have moments when we wonder why we are doing "this."

Beliefs, relationships, knowledge, experience, skills, and talents are all resources we have available to us. Anything you've ever seen or heard that has impacted you deeply is a resource you can call upon to help you do whatever it is you want to get done.

As you act on your commitment, you will begin to develop the confidence required to do the next thing. Your own why is one of your most important resources. Simon Sinek talks about the importance of why in his viral Ted Talk "Understand Your Why." I realized my why was for all those who were going through cancer, for those who couldn't do it, and also for those who were no longer here because of cancer.

Don't let what you can't do get in the way of what you can. I knew I would be riding for those who could no longer ride. I could ride in Ron's honor on the bike he gave me and for all those others who could no longer ride either because they'd lost their ability or because they were no longer around to do it. $41 million – that was the fundraising goal of the PMC just six short years ago – and last year they raised $56 million. This year the ride will have to be reimagined because of the global pandemic.

You think about taking up some massive project, such as running a marathon, climbing Mount Everest, or undertaking the Pan-Mass Challenge. Each and every year someone decides to do something extraordinary like that. They go through the same process I went through when I discovered that I could complete the Pan-Mass Challenge. You can only run a marathon one mile at a time, climb Mount Everest one step at a time, just like I could only complete the Pan-Mass Challenge one pedal stroke at a time. Of course, before you can run a marathon or climb Mount Everest, you have to prepare and you have to "commit" to getting there.

After you commit, you will make progress at your own pace. Sometimes it will be fast; sometimes it will be painstakingly slow. Sometimes, you will feel you can't do it alone, and that's not necessarily a bad thing. Any program requiring individuals to take action day by day, one day at a time, doesn't have to be done individually without assistance. Sometimes working with a partner works better.

Get an Accountability Partner

When I first started out, my friend Michael O'Brien (OB) was my accountability partner. OB is the survivor of a near death experience and he knows a thing or two about both cycling and accountability. As a matter of fact, he had his last bad day on July 11, 2001, and you can read all about it in his book Shift. If you really want to be successful, get an accountability partner. This is another resource. Your accountability partner is someone who demonstrates to you that you are not on this journey alone. Remember, "together we accomplish more." Put together a team that supports you in this process.

Although this book is being written lineally, your journey will not develop that way. You will be in and out of various parts of this process as you are on your journey.

If you have this really big idea and this really big plan and this really big thing you want to do, you also have a choice. You have the choice to either eliminate, or limit, the amount of time you spend around those who don't support you. Instead, align yourself with people who are interested in helping you or supporting you in doing what it is you want to do. Les Brown, a renowned motivational speaker talks about getting around OQP – Only Quality People.

If you're doing something you've never done before, it's going to be challenging. But if there are people who have done it before you, you know you can do it too. Success leaves tracks. Look for the tracks of success.

Jim Rohn says, "To teach is to learn twice." He goes on to say that when sharing information, both student and teacher are affected in the process. When the teacher shares, the student is affected, and in the process of sharing, so is the teacher. Mr. Rohn was a great storyteller. He had a way of pulling you into the conversation and getting you involved. He repeated key concepts, spoke slowly, enunciated clearly, and always gave prompts to encourage capturing the key concepts he shared.

He took teaching to the next level by continuously asking powerful questions and encouraging his audience not to believe him, but to investigate on their own. When discussing philosophy, for example, as it related to persistence, he used the ant to drive home the point.

He would ask us to think back when we were curious children and remember what we saw the ants doing. He would ask what happens when you place an object in the path of an ant? What does the ant do? How does the ant deal with the "obstacle?" An ant will always go around, over, or through any obstacle placed in front of it.

He then would ask, "And how long do you suppose an ant will try? The ant will try until... Until when? Until it succeeds, period!" Finally, he would ask, "What do you suppose might be the lesson here for all of us as it relates to the ants?"

Try until you succeed. You'll eventually get there, one day at a time.

Chapter Three: Manage Expectations

Early Lessons

I was exposed to the concept of expectations at an early age. It was winter. It was cold, and so was I. "Paper! Paper! Get your evening paper; read all about it." This was my mantra every day after school. I would come home and then head off to my job as a paperboy. In all but the worst of the weather in winter, I rode my bike to work. At eight years old I was too young to drive, but I didn't let that get in the way of my independence.

When the snow came, I relied on my mom for a ride to and from The Nugget, which is where I sold my daily allotment of papers. My mom and I had a deal about when it was and when it wasn't OK to call for a ride to be picked up from work. When I say "we," I really mean "she." I wasn't given the opportunity to offer my input as to how our deal should have been structured. Being raised by depression-era grandparents, I became used to rules that were a bit different than the rules for the rest of my friends. Grandma and Grandpa raised me. They were the only real parents I knew, so I just naturally called them Mom and Dad.

"Paper! Paper! Get your evening paper! Hey, Mister! Would you like to buy a paper?" Although we lived in Sparks, the paper I peddled daily was the Reno Evening Gazette, it was the local newspaper. As I handed the paper to my customer with my ever-present smile, I said, "Thank you, Mister!"

He said, "You're welcome. What a polite young man you are. Your parents must be mighty proud of you."

"Thanks," I said again. I believed they were mighty proud of me. I only knew of one way to converse with adults, and that was with respect.

It was getting late, and it was cold. It had started snowing some time ago and the flakes were not only sticking but accumulating as well. I loved to play in the snow, but I hated snow when selling papers. When it snowed, my paper sales always suffered. When it was cold, I suffered too. Sometimes it could take twice as long to sell all my papers when it snowed. It had been extra slow this day and I still had a lot of papers left. I began to get discouraged as the temperature continued to drop.

I went from discouraged to frustrated because I hadn't sold a single paper in the last half hour. People just kept pushing past me to get out of the wind and the cold. I started feeling invisible, as if they either didn't see me or didn't care.

Knowing it was probably a complete waste of time, I made the bold decision to call my mom to see if she would come pick me up. I stood on my tippy toes to put the money in the pay phone. Ching, ching. The nickels dropped into the coin collector on the phone. I held the receiver in my left hand shaking and shivering as I dialed home.

Rrrr,rrrr, was the sound as I put in each of the numbers. Ringggg, Ringgggg. I nervously waited for my mom to pick up. "Hello, Mom?"

"Yes, Bobby?" she replied.

"Mom, I'm rrrrealllly cccold, and I want to come home."

I heard the reply I was already dreading, "Bobby, have you sold all of your papers?"

"Well, nnnnoo, but I'm really cold and I want to come home, Mom!" Silence. Nothing. "Mom, Mom, did you hear me? I want to come home!"

"Yes, Bobby, I heard you. My hearing is perfect. What's our deal, Bobby?" she asked.

I sheepishly replied. "I don't call for a ride to come home until after I've sold all of my papers."

"That's correct," she said. "Have you sold all of your papers?"

"No, Mom," I replied, "but I'm freezing, and I want to come home!"

"Well then, I suggest you get creative and figure out a way to sell the rest of your papers as fast as you can. Goodbye, Son." I heard a click as she hung up on me.

I couldn't believe she hung up on me. I felt the tears welling up in my eyes and almost began to cry, but then I got mad and stomped my way all the way back to the main entrance where I sold my papers.

My mind was still trying to grasp what had just happened. As it began to sink in that Mom wasn't coming, I began to think about what she said, I suggest you get creative and figure out how to sell your papers as fast as you can.

Hmmm, I wondered. Well, it's worth a try, I thought to myself. I would normally put my shoulders back and do my best to hold my head high and proud. Instead, I hunched over a bit and waited for the next potential customer to come my way.

I moved out towards the gentleman approaching and said: "Hey, Mmmmister, yyyouu wanna bbbbuy a pppaper? As ssssoon as I sssselll all my ppppapers, I can ggggoo hhhhome."

Compassion filled the man's face. "Sure, Son, I'll help."

Wow, I thought. He wanted to help me! Well, that was very different than what I had been experiencing. I tried it again. Another one sold, two papers down, five more to go!

Then, I saw a lady coming. She was walking toward me with her cane. "Hi, Maam, you want to bbbuy a ppppaper?" I asked. "As soon as I sell the rrr-rest I can gggooo home."

"Sure, Sonny boy. How many papers do you have left to sell?" she asked.

"Ffffive," I replied.

"Give 'em all to me," she said. I was elated. I had sold all my papers. Now I could go call my mom and get a ride home. Just as I was getting ready to go back to the payphone, I heard a honk. I looked over my shoulder to see my mom pulling up to get me. I thought, "She hung up, but she came anyway."

The Measure of Expectations

"The ultimate measure of a man is not where he stands in moments of comfort and convenience, but where he stands at times of challenge and controversy."
-Martin Luther King Jr.

Dr. King was assassinated the year before I experienced my first lesson about managing expectations. I wish I could tell you I knew about what a great man and leader he was when I was 7, but the truth is, I barely remember him from my childhood.

I can tell you that, as an adult, I have been fascinated with everything I have been able to learn about this incredible man. As a matter of fact, I have a quote attributed to Dr. King on the living room wall in my home. It says, "I have decided to stick with love. Hate is too great a burden to bear."

When everything is going well, when life is good, when we are enjoying the fruits of our labor and basking in the glory of all that comes from a life of comfort and convenience, it's very easy to become complacent and forget about the struggle.

Each and every day throughout this great land and across the globe, there is struggle. When our values are challenged, we become immediately aware of just how close controversy can be. Where the struggle arises for most of us is in deciding what to do when facing a challenge or concern. This is where the measure comes in. Anyone can do nothing. Doing nothing is easy. Where it becomes a real challenge is when we stand up and say no more!

But what is just as important as standing up is the way we go about it. And this subtle distinction is what made Dr. Martin Luther King Jr. such a great leader. He led; he really led. His commitment to peaceful protest and the denunciation of all violence was the ultimate measure of him as a great man!

"The truth is incontrovertible."
-Winston Churchill

Dr. King found a way. Actually, he created a way when there seemed no way forward. He rallied not just some Americans, not just one race, not just one creed, not just one color. His message spoke to anyone willing to at least open their eyes and ears and engage with their own mind to think, to actually think, about what he was saying. And what he was saying was grounded in truth.

This is just one of the many lessons Dr. King gave us. He left behind for all of us who would follow, not just a legacy, but a road map of truth. He was the ultimate measure of a man. And fortunately, we have a record of his actions as a reference for how we can all be great citizens and exercise our own measures in times of challenge and controversy. From lessons like his, we learn about responsibility, commitment, and when to take action.

I didn't realize it at the time, I was too young. What I know now looking back on my time as a paperboy, is that when my grandma mom hung up on me, she was simply trying to teach me the best way she knew how. She was teaching me about responsibility, about commitment, and how to stand on my own. It was a hard lesson, but it served me well.

Expectations and Limits

> *"Everyone has limits. You just have to learn what your own limits are and deal with them accordingly."*
> *-Nolan Ryan*

If you have ever had any appreciation whatsoever for baseball, Nolan Ryan requires no introduction. For those who don't follow baseball, just know he is still considered to be one of the best pitchers of all time. He was known for his fast ball. What do you suppose a great pitcher might be trying to express about limits? What if you were expected to have a multitude of skills, varying pitches for example, and you were only fair at all the other pitches you were expected to know and throw? How do we deal accordingly with our own limits?

First, we must be willing to make an honest assessment or evaluation of our current skill level, strengths, abilities, and areas of opportunity, or what some refer to as weaknesses. To clarify, an area of opportunity only becomes a weakness when it's not acknowledged and managed.

Using this strategy, I was forced to take a hard look at where I was at the beginning of my training for the Pan-Mass Challenge. We must first know ourselves and we must decide if we are willing to put the work and the effort in to manage our limits. At the beginning of my training, I had many limits that were real and many more that were perceived. I decided I was willing to put in the work to face the real limits and as I did, some of my perceived limits began to diminish.

Whatever it is that you want to do that's important to you, then do it. Don't waste a bunch of time worrying about what you're not great at. Acknowledge it honestly. Not everyone can be great at everything, but we can each be great at something. Become great at the one thing you are really good at already. Develop excellence in the one thing and learn how to manage around your limits. One of the reasons teams are so effective is because each member has the opportunity to be great at their one thing and leverage the abilities of the rest of the team to manage their limitations in other areas. There's plenty for each of us to remember about leveraging both our abilities and the abilities of those around us.

What are some of the strategies to deal with limits effectively? In other words, what are the work arounds? First, we can get better. There isn't a book we can't read or a skill we can't learn. Remember, we don't need to be excellent at everything. The work around is to either become proficient, delegate the task to someone else, or manage around it. We can outsource. Let those who are experts bring their value to what we are trying to accomplish. Make them a part of the team.

How else can we manage around our limits? Answer creatively, and we can then focus on being the very best at whatever we are already really good at doing. Finally, let's not forget about coaches. Even the greatest pitchers in baseball have pitching coaches! Coaches see what we can't. Great coaches help us manage around our limits by helping us deal with them accordingly.

Terry from the bike shop wasn't my "official" coach, but he functioned in the same capacity. He also functioned as a mentor as did my colleagues who were experienced riders willing to share what they had learned as they prepared for their first PMC.

Expectations and Philosophy

"However much we guard ourselves against it, we tend to shape ourselves in the image others have of us. It is not so much the example of others we imitate, as the reflection of ourselves in their eyes and the echo of ourselves in their words."
-Eric Hoffer

Self-esteem is often related to the perception of others, which is incredibly intriguing if you look at the word on its own merit. Even when "we guard against it, we tend to shape ourselves in the image others have of us." This could work in our favor if we are referring to people who are trying to lift us. But what happens when that is not the case? Do we then fall prey to the pervasive attitudes and ideals of those who are most influential in our lives?

How do we develop a reflection of ourselves from the eyes of others? What words might they be using that would have us believing what they say versus what we believe about what's possible? Two views make all the difference. The first is the idea that you can do, be, or become whatever you are willing to commit to learning and becoming. The second is the one that questions your ability to do, be, or become, expressed as statements and questions like, "No one from around here has ever done anything like that before," and "You're not smart enough to," "Who do you think you are?" You get the idea.

We must guard our minds with the same level of vigilance we guard our children, or the same way a mother bear guards her cubs. We all know what happens if you get too close to bear cubs. Guard your mind! Be vigilant!

As I prepared to take on my very first Pan-Mass Challenge, I had some detractors. I had some non-believers and some doubters, but the biggest adversary I faced was the one in the mirror. As you take on whatever challenge you're facing, ignore the doubters and watch carefully the person in the mirror!

Expectations, Humility, And Mental Toughness

> *"Mental toughness is many things. It is humility because it behooves all of us to remember that simplicity is the sign of greatness and meekness is the sign of true strength. Mental toughness is spartanism with qualities of sacrifice, self-denial, dedication. It is fearlessness, and it is love."*
> *-Vince Lombardi*

If we do the things we know we need to do, even when we don't feel like doing them, then we are mentally tough. Being strong on the field or on the job doesn't mean strength is the only way. Being mentally tough is also being gentle when the situation calls for it. There is strength in meekness. Adaptability allows us to be and do so many things. We can be patient when required. We can find the simplest method to accomplish our goals. We can be meek when it might be much easier to be gruff or unkind.

We can be tough and maintain dedication to our beliefs and be gentle at the same time. We can be both fearless and loving. Sacrifice and self-denial are also part of the mental toughness spectrum, particularly relating to our presence on a team, or working toward a team or group goal. Mental toughness is about strength, the strength of mind; it's about making conscious decisions and taking massive action to support them. It's taking appropriate action for the situation at hand. It's the application of knowledge to our life. It's wisdom!

When riding the Pan-Mass Challenge, we ride together. We ride as a peloton of individuals all moving in the same direction for a unified cause. However, when we train, many of us train alone, whether it be on the road or on a cycling trainer in our living room at home. Mental toughness is riding alone whether you feel like it or not. It's getting up when the alarm goes off and not hitting the snooze button. As you face your own individual challenges, you will have to avoid the snooze button and embrace sacrifice and self-denial.

Expectations and Difficulty

"What is difficulty? Only a word indicating the degree of effort required to accomplish something! A mere notice of the necessity for exertion; a scarecrow to children and fools and a stimulus to real men."
-Samuel Warren

When I first began cycling, hills were really hard. As I became more experienced, I shifted my attitude about hills. Along the way, I began to see the hills as difficult instead of hard. The hills didn't change; they were the same. However, my attitude toward the hills was different. Eventually, I changed the language to challenging, and when I did, hills were no longer hard or difficult.

When a task is hard to accomplish, understand, or deal with, we tend to label it difficult. We typically use the word difficulty to describe or refer to a problem, a situation that is dangerous, or an obstacle. No matter how the word is used, it is just a word. As a matter of fact, the word has no real value other than the value we assign it.

Our own individual realization or perception is what determines whether something is or isn't difficult. How else can you explain the variances of what people describe as difficult or challenging? Why is it easy for one person to get up in front of a large group and speak freely, and the next person struggles to find their words? What if these two were the same person? That's the difference between a person who gets stuck dealing with their struggle and a person who once struggled but doesn't anymore.

Who gets to determine the degree of effort required for a specific task? What's the difference between the words we use and the pictures we create in our mind to justify the difficulty of a specific task or supposed challenge? Why is quitting smoking, for example, easy for some and almost impossible for others? What about a new skill or ability? A new language? The ability to learn a musical instrument?

Where does the word exertion or effort come into play? What emotions or feelings do we associate with the words? What if we associate pain with exertion? What if we associate pleasure with exertion, instead of pain? What if we view exertion and difficulty as stimulating? Our perception is more important than any potential degree of difficulty associated with any situation or challenge.

Expectations and Balance

"Balance activity with serenity, wealth with simplicity, persistence with innovation, community with solitude, familiarity with adventure, constancy with change, leading with following."
-Jonathan Lockwood Huie

Deep within each of us is a center or point of balance. This point of balance is based on all of the information we have taken in over our lifetime. Everything we have learned, everything we have been told, everything we have seen, everything we have come to know is stored in this place. We often call it or refer to it as our experience.

find visual images best for explaining new concepts. For the purpose of his exercise, I would ask you to consider a teeter-totter. Why? Balance! Don't just consider the fulcrum point on which the teeter-totter pivots. Consider the images we can retrieve by simply thinking of our childhood schoolyard, playground, or park. There is power in these images if we harness them. Remember the childhood image I described earlier when sharing my paperboy experience? Our lives are full of these types of images. Unfortunately, most of us haven't been taught how to use and apply this recall ability.

For a teeter-totter to function effectively, there must be a relative balance on each side of the teeter-totter. For life to function effectively, there must be a relative balance between the various demands life places on us. The teeter-totter will still function if somewhat out of balance, just as life will, but it takes a lot of extra energy to do so.

Balance is the place from which our habits arise. Both our desirable and undesirable habits develop either in, or out of, balance. Many of the things we do, we simply "do." It isn't until we pause long enough to ask why that we can even begin to understand some of our basic behaviors. We may not have any real understanding of why we are either doing or not doing a specific task until we make time for this pause. The simplest way to discover an answer is to ask yourself a question, preferably an empowering question. Empowering questions are open-ended questions that lead us to solutions, like asking "What could I have done better?" instead of "Why do I always fail?"

Nutrition and exercise are two areas we can easily evaluate by asking empowering questions to uncover behavior patterns and habit thinking versus conscious contemplation. We are all well aware of the importance of nutrition and exercise. As a matter of fact, we are probably more aware of these facts than we have ever been in the history of developed culture. Why then are we facing an epidemic of obesity in America? What gives? What is missing from the equation of knowledge?

The answer is balance. We are simply not balancing our knowledge with choice. Knowing something is not enough; we must also act. When we act with balance, we can make more informed choices, more informed deci sions. It is the balance of activity with relaxation that leads to healthier choices. It is the balance of smaller portions and not all out denial that leads to smarter choices. Understanding is not enough, either; we must also consciously acknowledge the results of our choices.

When I began my training for the Pan-Mass Challenge, I was at least 20 pounds overweight. I knew that to get in the shape necessary to accom plish what I chose to do, I would have to make some changes in my eating habits. The good news was I only had to focus on the eating because the exercise part was happening as a result of my training. I set an expectation to start releasing a couple of pounds a week, nothing crazy. It would have been overwhelming If I had become obsessed with losing the weight be fore I got serious about training. Instead, my expectation was in alignment with my action and the pounds slowly disappeared.

We must first decide what it is we actually want, and when our "why" is clear, then consciously choose the activities that will support our desired results. Without a compelling "why," we will almost certainly fail. Willpow er alone is not enough to override our habits.

Conscious choice is only ever made when we are consciously aware. Con scious choices are readily made in the absence of other easier, more tempt ing choices that require no discipline. Is it possible to replace our less than desirable habits with conscious choices? Of course it is! Conscious choices are exactly how we begin the process of regaining balance.

Life is a spectrum with extremes at either end, and in the middle, there is balance. The experience of life has the potential to be whatever we make of it. What benefits might be available to us with a more balanced life? We have a need for both constancy and change. We value both familiarity and adventure. Some choose to lead in certain areas and follow in others. Is it possible to live both a simplistic and a wealthy life? What is real wealth anyway? It certainly isn't just monetary! It is the combination of ideas and experiences that makes for a rich life.

When we balance activity with serenity, work with play, and desire with discipline, we take control of our lives and create a balanced state. Balanced activity is nothing more than conscious creation. It is consciously choosing to do certain things and then simply doing them.

All we have any real control over is our own thoughts. We regain balance the moment we acknowledge the truth of this fact, and we regain our power the moment we act on this realization. We each have the capacity and the capability to regain balance. However, with all of the demands of life, at some points in life balance may not be available. In that case, choose harmony. Harmony is available to all of us because harmony begins in the mind.

There are many things we can't control in life, but our thinking is not one of them. We can set an expectation to consciously manage our thoughts. Our mind is like a gate. We get to control what we let in, and we take control with the choices we make. Stand guard at the gate of your mind.

Expectations and Preparation

"You had better live your best and act your best and think your best today; for today is the sure preparation for tomorrow and all the other tomorrows that follow."
-Helen Martineau

We can only ever really live in the moment. Everything else is just preparation for the exact moment we are experiencing as we experience it. We can't live in the future. We can plan for tomorrow, but we can't live there.

Whatever it is you want to achieve or accomplish, it will only be experienced in the moment. Every wrong attempt discarded is a moment. Every failure is a moment. Every victory is a moment. Moments add up over time, day by day, one day at a time. It is the accumulation of our moments of preparation behind the scenes that prepare us to experience our bigger wins in real time.

Every training ride I completed was a moment behind the scenes in preparation for the event itself. I started slow. I knew I couldn't go from 0 to 192 overnight or even in a month. I set my expectations high but approached each day as it came. I did my best not to get too far ahead of myself. Patience became both a friend and an ally. I recommend making friends with patience. It will become your strongest ally!

There are several examples of individuals living out this constant challenge of both planning for the future and living in the moment. One of the most common examples is the athlete as either an individual or part of a team.

Let's first look at the "preparation" for what at first glance appears to be an individual athlete, a sprinter. One of the most famous sprinters in recent history is Usain Bolt from Jamaica. In an interview after one of his "victories" he told the reporter, "Winning was the easy part; all of the real work was behind the scenes in the daily grind of preparation." Usain Bolt, most famously known for his individual effort, was also an integral part of the Jamaican Relay Team victory as well.

Most of us have enjoyed an epic presentation on the big screen at one time or another. When a film is made, there are hundreds of moving parts involved at any given moment, all of which are leading up to the moment the cameras are rolling, and the scene is captured for us to enjoy later after editing. All of the work, all of the preparation, is for that one moment when the director says, "ACTION!"

Our own lives play out the same as both examples given. All of the effort takes place behind the scenes but comes to fruition in a single defining moment we refer to as the present. The only way we can ever be the very best we are capable of becoming is by preparing for the present. We either shine or fail in the defining moment. However, failure doesn't actually occur in the moment for most people. It has already occurred in all of the moments leading up to that moment, when the opportunity for practice and preparation was pushed to the side for something easier or more exciting than the disciplined effort required for long term success.

Discipline doesn't just mean doing the things we know we should be doing even when we don't feel like doing them. No, discipline is also the ability to say no to the things that aren't moving us in the direction of our desired outcome. Remember, we are always either moving toward or away from our desired outcome at any given point in time. Discipline is the ability to say no to the hundreds of distractions, while focusing on and preparing for what we have decided is most important to us, both individually and collectively, in the present.

To make sure we are properly prepared for tomorrow, for our next step, we plan ahead of time the activities we believe will best support our efforts to be fully present and prepared when tomorrow arrives. When we live our best, act our best, and think our best today, we are making a commitment to be our best tomorrow when it is looming in front of us asking, "Are you prepared for the opportunity of 'today'?"

It is our day-to-day mundane and monotonous preparation which affords us the opportunity to be our best both tomorrow and all of the other to-morrows as they unfold day by day and become present. Be your best; do your best; be prepared!

Expectations and Grit

"Consistency of effort over the long run is EVERYTHING."
-Angela Duckworth

Grit, by Angela Duckworth, was both a resource and a reminder of the importance of my expectations. When her book was released in 2016, I voraciously consumed it as I was already in preparation mode for the PMC ride that year. It confirmed everything I had discovered on my journey of preparation and how I was prepared to show up for the experience of the actual event my first year two years before. I would have never succeeded without all those hours of practice, without consistency of effort.

I can almost assure you the majority of all of the unbelievably passion-ate golfers of the world did not start out being passionate about golf. As a matter of fact, the majority of golfers started out being frustrated and perplexed. However, they learned the fundamentals, developed an under-standing, and realized that golf is a game of opposites through constant practice. This is exactly how it unfolded for me as I learned the game as well. Golf has humbled some of the greatest athletes of the world. Many a great athlete has been forced to change and manage their expectations of proficiency. I too adjusted my expectations of the game. I am what you might call a recreational golfer. I now play for the pure joy of it.

As the beginning golfer learns the basics of GPA, -- Grip, Posture, and Alignment -- they also begin to realize they can learn the game. This is the same paradigm for almost any new endeavor we know absolutely nothing about. We can plug in just about anything we can think of and draw a cor-relation between a person learning to play golf and a person learning any new hobby, like how to play the piano, learn skills, apps, selling strategies, computer programs, painting, dance, cycling, and anything else we haven't completely mastered, up to and including, yes, even our work. Passion is something we can develop over the long run.

"Grit," as Angela Duckworth explains it, is the ability to find the thing that will sustain your interest, even when it gets hard and boring. The author describes "grit" as a dogged tenacity to succeed. How do we develop it? By learning any characteristic we admire and don't yet completely know or understand. Passionate, patient, persistent learning leads to "grit."

Chapter Four: Make Mistakes...And Friends, Too

The Gifts of Failure

When I went out for my first long ride in preparation for the PMC, I entertained an internal conversation with myself as I contemplated the idea of giving up. The pain was excruciating. I wasn't just cramping; my legs were spasming. It wasn't just my calves either; my whole legs were involved. Both of them!

First, I tried to walk it off; then I was on my back writhing in pain. The spasms wouldn't stop. As I was experiencing all of this, a negative conversation began in my head; my brain was screaming, Why are you doing this to yourself? What are you trying to prove? This is stupid! This is ridiculous!

The other voice in my head, the one that originally said yes to the PMC said, You know why we're doing this. Don't be ridiculous!

The me that was in pain replied, Oh, so now I'm ridiculous? What's ridiculous is thinking I could ever get in "good enough" shape to do a 192-mile bike ride. That's what's ridiculous!

The other voice in my head replied, Now you're just whining. Stop complaining and suck it up. Stop your damn whining! What, are you a quitter?

Well, are you? Are you a quitter?

Hey, hey boy, I'm talking to you! Are you a quitter? You gonna give up? You wanna run home to your mama?" Drill Sergeant Revelle? I swear I heard him yelling at me. Basic training was almost thirty years ago. How the hell did he get in my head? There it is again, Get up private! Let's go. We're gonna run till I get tired. This ain't no picnic! Ain't no discharge on the ground. Let's go!

What the hell is happening? I thought. Most of the time when we are faced with extreme difficulty, we have a tendency to look outside ourselves for the answer. The answer to my current challenge was INSIDE me! It was rooted deep in my past, but it was there. It was in the voice of my drill sergeant, the one who had turned me into a man ready to lay down his life for his country, the one who had taught me that when we thought we were done, we were nowhere close to done.

When I was in basic training, I watched Drill Sergeant Revelle turn mere boys into men, and now he was in my head to remind me I had inside me everything I could ever need to do anything I ever wanted to accomplish.

I said back to the voice of Drill Sergeant Revelle, Hell no, I ain't no quitter and I'm sure as hell not running home to my momma!

I worked out the cramps and I got back on that bike. It was slow at first and then, as my legs began to work again, a familiar sound came rolling into my subconscious. It was the sound of cadence. Drill Sergeant Revelle was still with me taking me home.

Here we go, here we go, all the way, all the way, every day, every day, one step, one step, two steps, two steps, stepping out, stepping out, running now, running now, here we go, here we go, all the way, all the way!

And then I picked it up in my mind. I don't know but I've been told Bobby Kountz is good as gold; I don't know but I've been told, Bobby Kountz is good as gold!

Then another one came into my head, C-130 rolling down the strip, Airborne trooper gonna take a little trip. Stand-up, hook-up, shuffle to the door, jump right out on a count of four. If my main don't open wide, I got a reserve by my side. If that one should fail me too, look out, ground, I'm coming through... I was back on the road and the still small voice within had won. I'd made it!

Mistakes and failures are gifts. When we take the time to learn from our mistakes and failures, we are able to tap into resources either we forgot we had or which only become available to us through our willingness to evaluate our experience with the intention to grow and learn.

Learning from our mistakes is an essential skill for our own personal growth and development. It allows us to move forward, stay positive, and develop qualities and characteristics like resilience, determination, and persistence. When we learn, we take ownership of our experience; we recognize the mistakes as an opportunity to begin again in a different direction and with additional information.

One of the greatest gifts we can ever give ourselves is the gift of failure. If we ever hope to be successful at anything, we must first give ourselves permission to make mistakes and permission to fail miserably. One of the surest ways to figure out how to do something right is to do it wrong. Part of the challenge is that we live in a world obsessed with success. We have literally been socialized into thinking mistakes are somehow bad. It's sheer nonsense.

The reason many people shy away from trying new things or taking risks is an underlying fear of failure. Another common form or subtle type of fear many of us experience is "what if" thinking. The majority of "what if" thinking is negative in nature. A common example of one of the thoughts we may experience is, What if I'm not good enough?

Almost every "what if" thought we might experience will come from some form of an underlying I'm-not-good-enough-based thought expressed as a "what if" question we pose to our subconscious mind.

Here are some examples for your consideration: What if I'm too old? What if I don't have the patience to finish what I start? What if I'm not smart enough? What if I don't train hard enough? What if all of the other demands of my already busy life get in the way? This was one of mine.

The "what if" list of things that could potentially go wrong is rather extensive. Stop and think for a minute. Ask yourself about some of your own what if's. Now, let's flip the script! Ask yourself instead: What if it all goes right? What if it all works out? What if I am smart enough, determined enough, good enough? What if?

How You Handle Those Who Don't Support You

You have to set clear boundaries with the people who aren't willing to get behind you in the cause. You are going to have to make a decision, at some point, as to what is more important to you, the commitment you've made to doing what you want to do or pleasing someone who isn't aligned with your why.

Accept the fact that you will probably upset someone if you choose to do something you've never done before. The bigger the task you want to achieve, the higher the probability you will run into resistance with friends, family, or a loved one.

Consider carefully how you are going to do that yourself when you take on something you've never done before. You will probably end up alienating someone who can't see it with you in the beginning. You may speak to someone in a manner that you wish you hadn't spoken to them. You may do something that you regret. You're going to make mistakes along the way, and you need to be able to reconcile that. You need to be able to acknowledge that it was a mistake. You wish you had done it differently. You can't change it because it's in the past.

It's important to make these mistakes and to also make friends along the way that can be impartial observers, who can help you get an objective perspective on what you're feeling guilty about and help you figure out how to move forward in the direction you want to go.

There's a gap between where you are and where you want to be. In that gap is the feeling of guilt or shame. Those feelings are what's keeping you safe and small. You have to be able to look at them and move through them so you can rise to your highest calling.

Remember that those who are closest to us may not have the capacity to support us. Oftentimes our friends and loved ones are operating from their own limited perspective of what they believe is possible and simply can't see what we see because they don't have the dream or idea that we have. It's not their fault.

Tom Bilyeu has a YouTube video, titled Nothing Can Hold You Back, where he discusses the fact that the people who are closest to us often don't support us because they can't see what we see, and they don't have the capacity to see it.

Be Grateful Anyway

"Gratitude is the inward feeling of kindness received. Thankfulness is the natural impulse to express that feeling. Thanksgiving is the following of that impulse."
-Henry Van Dyke

Gratitude is one of the most powerful forces available to mankind. With gratitude, we can accomplish unimaginable things. Gratitude literally unlocks the storehouse of possibilities. How can we describe the inward feeling of kindness received? Some might call it fulfillment; others might call it something different; this author calls it "joy."

I am a self-described gratitude addict. I have so many different reasons to be thankful. I truly believe gratitude is the cure for what ails the world. Well, it's really a combination of gratitude, attitude, and mindset. Oh, and did I mention curiosity? Curiosity is a superpower! The world would be a completely different place if everyone were curious instead of judgmental.

"Be curious, not judgmental."
-Walt Whitman

Gratitude led me to develop a friendship with Chris Palmore, the founder and Chief Gratitude Officer at Gratitude Space. Chris is an amazing human being with a heart of gold. He is another person I met in the digital world who has become a real friend.

Chris's mission is to bring the world closer together by sharing gratitude on his blog. He has interviewed hundreds of influencers who have openly shared their messages of gratitude. Recently, I was able to connect Chris with a couple of people to interview, and we regularly help and support one another with projects. Remember, "Make friends too."

No matter what we call it, the desire or the natural impulse to express the feeling associated with gratitude is, as stated in the quote, "thankfulness." The sensation we experience of wanting to reciprocate and express the warm feeling deep in the fiber of our being and expressed in the fabric of our soul is thankfulness. The act, the actual act of expressing our gratitude to another human being, is the following of the impulse and the expression of that impulse with words that somehow seem to fall immeasurably short of expressing what we really feel.

However inadequate our words may seem, we must still make the effort to express them in the best way we can because gratitude of the heart unexpressed is like a gift beautifully wrapped but never presented. It has no real value. The value only makes itself known to us and others when expressed. It is only in the expression of our gratitude, through the action of thanksgiving, that both we and the recipient experience the magic of joy that gratitude brings to life.

Friends Are Like Windows

"Each friend represents a world in us, a world possibly not born until they arrive, and it is only by this meeting that a new world is born."
-Anais Nin

When two people come together in friendship, in conversation, there is a special connection that develops through the power of words. The words shared in conversation are like a bridge between the thoughts of the individuals conversing, thus allowing for creativity and connection that otherwise would not exist. Sometimes these words open up not just new worlds, but entire galaxies.

This is what happened when I met my friend and author, Steve Bivans. We both knew almost immediately we had a lot in common. We were fully engaged in multiple conversations on a new audio app called Anchor.

Soon after, Steve had decided he was going to write a book on "fear." I told him I would do whatever I could to help. I'm not really a fan of social media and, to this day, other than the time I spent on Anchor, the only platform I ever spent much time on was Twitter because I discovered a really supportive writing community there.

As Steve continued to talk about the book he was writing, I began to believe that maybe, just maybe, I could write a book, too. After all, I actually had a really great idea for a book. I was already writing my daily inspirational messages. It didn't seem that far of a stretch for me. Writing a daily message is nothing like writing a book. This was a lesson I would learn over time as I struggled to write the book you are now reading.

Before long, Steve and I were discussing his book on a regular basis. I started sharing ideas and resources with him. He began coaching me on the book writing process. Whenever he was struggling with a concept, we would figure out a way together to get through it.

I remember introducing Steve to the work of Noah St. John and his Book of Afformations. Steve thought I was giving him a resource for his book; he didn't know at the time I thought maybe Noah's book could help him with some of his "head trash."

We hear the word "friend" used in many different ways. An individual writing a book or article may refer to their intended readers as friends. We hear people on both the radio and television refer to listeners and watchers as friends on a regular basis. We have peers, colleagues, fellow workers, virtual friends, and complete strangers, all of whom make up our realm of friends and potential friends. Each of them has the capacity to open up a whole new world for us by simply sharing a little bit of who they are and what is important to them.

The writer, for example, may introduce us to stories we had never even considered. A poet might show us how words can be woven together to evoke thought and emotion. A music lover or musician may open their world of appreciation or talent to us and we might suddenly find ourselves enjoying their world through their experience and expression. In friends, we find both common ground and undiscovered territories. Through an acquaintance we might learn of culture and lifestyle in a distant land. Their world is opened up to us through their sharing and description of their experience.

This was the experience of the Anchor Audio App in the early days of Version 1.0. I met writers, music lovers, and musicians, a poet from Cork, Ireland, another writer from Dublin. I met artists, fitness experts, even a super cool former lawyer turned philosopher named Patrick. It was an amazing experience. I met a whole new world of virtual friends with mutual interests.

I had several conversations with one of the coolest individuals I haven't had a chance to meet in person yet. Her name is Barbara J. Faison, and she is the author of Why Struggle? Life Is Too Short To Wear Tight Shoes. The book encourages us to accept life for what it is – an unpredictable journey. Her book taught me to slow down and to think about how I would create my own adventure much the same way kids naturally seem to do.

New worlds are revealed to us through the gifts of our acquaintances and friendships. Each friend may expose us to a world we may, as of yet, not know. We may come to learn of pain and suffering and peace and happiness. We may learn of sorrow and joy. We may learn of light and dark. We may learn of love and hate. We might experience a sense of profound connection or be repelled beyond expectation.

We might find, in a friend, a mirror that reflects back to us exactly what we are doing within ourselves, or we might find a bold new world of technology and innovation we didn't even know existed. When we reach out to another human being, there is no way for us to know for sure what we will get, but we can be sure it will be a world that, had we not reached out, might not have been made available to us. The gift received is the world opened up to us by the person we would dare to call our friend.

I dared to call Steve my friend and, in time, we met in real life. We are still friends today even though he lives in the frigid midwest of Minnesota and I live in the sweltering desert of Las Vegas. Steve has been an incredible inspiration and resource for me. I've learned from him and his book The End of Fear Itself.

Enthusiasm and Friends

"Enthusiasm releases the drive to carry you over obstacles and adds significance to all you do."
-Norman Vincent Peale

Whenever we are committed to doing something of significance, we can be assured of one thing: We will encounter obstacles. We will always encounter obstacles. The energy of "enthusiasm" will carry us over, around, or through the obstacles we face.

When we make a commitment to make the difference we know we are capable of making in the world, it is our enthusiasm that will carry us over our hurdles. Once we decide to embrace a challenge, we will discover within ourselves all of the energy and persistence required to achieve our desired outcome.

There are as many different reasons for doing the things we do as there are ways of doing them. Some of the requirements of our work are relatively simple. Some elements are much more challenging. If we are in customer service, it is expected that we do our best to make sure customers experience great service. If we are in sales, we will be expected to make sales. If we provide a service, it is expected that we provide that service to the best of our ability.

Enthusiasm allows us to do things just a little bit differently. When we embrace enthusiasm, we have the ability to get in touch with the bigger reason driving us to be our best. For some, it's the simple satisfaction of knowing they have done their best. For others, it may be knowing they are making a real difference.

One person who knows they are making a real difference is Brandy Miller. She is my friend. The way Brandy makes a difference is by helping people interested in telling their stories find the words that will best express the ideas they most want to share with their readers. This book only exists because I was smart enough to make Brandy a part of my team.

I knew from my experience of preparing for and completing the PMC I would have a much better chance of writing and publishing my book with a team behind me. I had also witnessed my friend OB go through the process of writing his book and took lessons from him as he went through the experience and shared with me how he had assembled his book writing "peloton."

I also had the experience of seeing a book created in real time as I supported my friend Steve through the process of writing The End of Fear Itself. He will be the first one to tell you that without his editor, his books would be garbage. Brandy was initially my writing coach and helped with editing and formatting. Between her and Steve, I finally began to understand the importance of "story."

I have read so many business, personal growth, and self-help books that I somehow forgot just how important the power of story is. Some personal development books are better at capturing stories than others. It became my hope that I could learn this skill so my readers would be more engaged with the messages I ultimately wanted to share, messages that I was sure would help them create the kind of lives they always knew they could live.

Some are fortunate enough to know the difference they make can be the difference between life and death. Some of us champion movements or causes. There are many causes committed to helping others. Some are even committed to eradicating disease, saving lives, or somehow improving overall health.

The enthusiasm with which we carry on our conversations with others has a real impact on what they ultimately think and believe. Passion is often palpable, and passion combined with knowledge, persistence, determination, and enthusiasm becomes a force to be reckoned with. We each make the difference we are capable of making when we commit to doing so.

This book wasn't written during the current crisis the world is now facing. However, it was being edited and prepared for publication during this time, so I added this story to honor not just the current crisis the American people are facing, but also the systemic racism and inequality that has plagued our great nation for hundreds of years.

As a writer, creative, artist, I can no longer stand by and not use the power gifted me. I have the ability to express myself with the simple use of words, and although I may not be a well-known writer, that doesn't make my voice any less important. As a matter of fact, because I am not a well-known writer, the responsibility rests squarely on my shoulders to encourage every other individual with a voice to speak up and stop hiding behind the security of white privilege.

The influential voices of my earliest years were silenced forever the same way thousands of other voices have been silenced across America over the years. In the first decade of my life, three of the greatest voices of that time were silenced. On November 22, 1963, the first voice was silenced. On April 4, 1968, the second voice was silenced. And just to make sure the dream that had been building and growing across the land would be crushed forever, the third voice was silenced on June 6, 1968. It's time for the silence to stop.

I'm not suggesting some grand conspiracy. I'm simply stating dates and facts. I will leave the conspiracy conversation to the theorists and speculators. It should be noted, however, that the leadership of our country at the time was moving in the right direction to bring about the change our great nation so desperately needed. This change was not popular with many of the people in power who were threatened by the idea of equality. This change has been slow and, at times, almost imperceptible over the last five decades. Its time has finally come.

On May 25, 2020, a date which will live in infamy, America watched the culmination of hundreds of years of oppression come to a sudden and traumatic conclusion as George Floyd gasped for breath in the video that captured a Minneapolis police officer kneeling on his neck for over eight minutes while George pleaded for his very life and other officers stood by and watched.

In the civil unrest that naturally unfolded after this horrific incident, the leader of our nation was absent. As the peaceful protests grew, as they naturally should in a country built on a promise of freedom and justice for all, instead of providing leadership for the country, our leader employed jackboot tactics reminiscent of the the Nazi oppressive regime that silenced millions.

Peaceful protesters outside the White House exercising their constitutional rights were suddenly and deliberately attacked by forces of the government. The entire incident was captured on video, and as the world watched the movement grew. Demonstrations began in other countries across the globe in solidarity with the protesters in America.

No one is claiming George Floyd was a saint. What the protesters are simply claiming is that he was a human being and that's all that matters.

The hope that once existed in this great country, the dream of an America "deeply rooted in the American Dream, the dream that one day this nation will rise up and live out the true meaning of its creed: -- we hold these truths to be self-evident, that all men are created equal," that dream, a dream delayed but not forgotten, has been reborn. It's a shame it has taken so long and it's a shame it had to come at such a costly price.

Life is a journey full of struggle and hope, and this book is all about both. We are the culmination of each and every one of our lived experiences, and this book is about both personal experiences and about what's possible when we make a commitment to make the difference only we, based on our experiences, make in the world.

This book provides a roadmap of possibilities that exist for the individual who is willing to make a commitment to achieve or accomplish whatever is important to them and take them from wherever they are at this current moment in time to exactly where they want to be systematically and methodically, one day at a time.

Let's all commit to making the difference only we are capable of making. By doing so, we will each, in our own small way, make the world just a little better, a little more significant, a little brighter! Individually we accomplish much; together we accomplish more, much more.

Mistakes and the Unknown

"Am I willing to give up what I have in order to be what I am not yet? Am I able to follow the spirit of love into the desert? It is a frightening and sacred moment. There is no return. One's life is charged forever. It is the fire that gives us our shape."
-Mary Caroline Richards

We each have, to varying degrees, a part of ourselves that is both addicted to some form of external love and afraid of failure at some level. I believe this is simply our ego either trying to protect us or prevent us from getting hurt or being rejected.

The love seeking part of ourselves that goes external comes from some form of foundational belief that love is discovered somewhere outside of ourselves. Here is the rub, though: Getting love from or through our achievements, possessions, other people, food, alcohol, or whatever else is just part of the underlying symptom or belief that we are not quite good enough and that love is somehow separate from who we are at our very core.

As I was writing this book, I was exposed to the work of the former comedian turned inspirational speaker and author, Kyle Cease. His revelations and his work, along with what I have learned from him, have been eye opening and transformational. In his book I Hope I Screw This Up, I was exposed to the concept of vulnerability and openness at a completely different level than I had previously experienced.

One of his most profound concepts, though, is the idea of "deep down." Most of us have probably heard the expression "deep down, I knew everything was going to be alright," or "deep down, I knew I could accomplish more than I had up until now," or "deep down, _____" and fill in the blank. Then Kyle asked a brilliant question, "What if we could live in 'deep down' all the time?"

He went on to explain the concept of embracing life from a place of not knowing what was going to happen and still being ok with whatever unfolded. This was another brilliant concept and confirmation for what I had discovered while uncovering my COMMITS pathway to progress. I had no idea where all of this was going to take me, but I knew I was very excited by the endless possibilities.

How different would our lives be if we declared, "I don't know exactly what life has in store for me and I love that" or "I know I don't exactly know how to do this thing I want to do, but that's ok, and I love that"?

> ***"Now faith is the substance of things hoped for, the evidence of things not seen."***
> ***-Hebrews 11:1***

Here's a what-if for you: What if we chose to just believe everything will simply work out as it will and whatever that is, it's OK?

Mistakes and Achievement

> ***"What a man really wants is creative challenge with sufficient skills to bring him within the reach of success so that he may have the expanding joy of achievement."***
> ***-Fay B. Nash***

We have a natural desire, as human beings, to creatively express ourselves.

I believe we also have an innate desire to solve or create solutions for the challenges or struggles that naturally manifest in our daily lives. A brief examination of our history demonstrates that we have been interested in solving the riddles and puzzles of life for literally thousands of years. We are born with an inquisitive nature that appears to be hard wired into our brains.

Our ability to think, combined with our instincts for survival and several other elements of our personality, is what keeps us constantly looking for opportunities to challenge ourselves creatively. We only appreciate, and even enjoy, difficult challenges when we have sufficient skills to deal with the circumstances of those challenges and the ability to either create or discover a solution to the challenges we face.

What's most interesting is that we don't even need or require skills sufficient enough to actually reach success. We just want to have skills enough to let us be either in, or a part of, the game. Now, there are some who view winning as a dichotomy. They believe if they are not winning, they must be losing. There are others who aren't necessarily interested in winning, but they do want to show up and play full out. They are happy to be playing the game and know that sometimes the actual destination is reached and sometimes progress is made toward it.

The most interesting group, though, in my opinion, is the collective body of individuals who say to themselves, How can we figure out a way for everyone to win? They often come together in small groups, referred to as teams, for the purpose of combining their efforts to compliment one another's abilities in their quest for creative solutions.

They see problems as opportunities for improvement. They often even say things like, "There are no problems, but only opportunities." Their mindset is that of inquiry and curiosity. While they will attempt to resolve a challenge, they also realize that having the skills and abilities to address the challenge is just as important as solving the challenge. They realize that an opportunity for expanding joy exists in each of the steps leading up to the resolution of the current challenge they face.

They become as excited with the prospect of solving the challenge as they are when the challenge is actually resolved. They experience the joy of the process. They are excited by the development of their own creative capacity. Achievement is viewed not as an end result but a joyful part of the experience.

Whether it is solving a simple jigsaw puzzle or solving a complex multi-faceted challenge a company is facing, we actually get inspired not by solving the problem, but by the pleasure of knowing we have sufficient skills to potentially solve it. We develop our skills as we grow, and we overcome challenges and difficulties we face as they naturally appear in our lives.

Preparing for and completing the PMC was both a puzzle and a challenge. Writing a book that will stand the test of time, be a real resource to another human being, have the potential to show readers they are smarter and better than they have given themselves credit for, allow the reader to realize that transformation is possible and a challenge, but a rewarding one. Taking a reader from where they are and transporting them to where they want to be is a gift and an achievement, and it can be done both in fiction and in real life.

Mistakes, Dedication, and Determination

"The price of success is hard work, dedication to the job at hand, and the determination that whether we win or lose, we have applied the best of ourselves to the task at hand."
-Vince Lombardi

Hard work is doing all that is required behind the scenes that allows us to be the very best we can be when we are in the light. With hard work, we can achieve success. Success can only ever be defined by the individual. Each of us have our own idea of success, whether it be long term in life or short term for a given goal. For one, it may be becoming rich; for another, it may be finishing school; for another, it may be overcoming a disease; for me, it was staying sober or completing the bike ride. We are the only ones who know if we have played full out. Only we can determine whether we were fully present in the moment and solely focused on the task at hand.

Most of the time, we only get to see the fruits of the efforts of those that make things look so easy when they are in the light. What we almost never see are the countless hours that go into the preparation of being or becoming ready. The level of commitment made by the individual to study and practice often determines the level of presentation or performance. The more dedicated a person is, the more likely they are to succeed. Dedication is showing up and doing your very best when you don't even feel like showing up at all.

Dedication is a quality of the highest nature. It is the quality of commitment, the quality of being committed to a desired outcome, task, activity, goal, or purpose. Determination is the quality that helps us continue trying to do or achieve something that is known or understood to be difficult. Determination is a decision that says we can and we will, and very simply, we will continue with our best effort. And if, in the end, we have not been victorious, we can look back proudly knowing that we gave it everything because we gave the very best we had to give and that is all there is.

Friends and Encouragement

"Encouragement is awesome. Think about it: It has the capacity to lift a man's or woman's shoulders. To spark the flicker of a smile on the face of the discouraged child. To breathe fresh fire into the fading embers of a smoldering dream."
-Charles Swindoll

Encouragement is one the most heartfelt actions we can engage in. When we give another human being support, endeavor to instill confidence, or simply help them see and feel that hope exists, we have given one of the greatest gifts possible. A little bit of encouragement given at the right time can be the difference between a person giving up or finding the courage and strength to persevere. Whether the method we use to encourage another is urging and prompting or through inspiration and incentive, it matters not. What matters is that we take the time to listen, engage, and ultimately encourage.

The word "encourage" is from the French, en-courage, and literally means to put courage into. By giving our support or advice, we have the ability, simply with our words, to literally give someone the courage to continue or to believe. We have the ability to encourage them to believe that what they are striving for is possible, and not just possible, but possible for them.

Our testimony can make all the difference and be the last piece of the puzzle that inspires belief, growth, and change. With our words, with the power of our words, when we take the time to say something and say it well, we literally can breathe life back into a project or a dream. We can help another to see what they previously could not. We can help them to believe what they previously did not. We can help them achieve that which they previously thought impossible. Yes, encouragement is awesome! I challenge you to pause for a moment and think about who you can encourage today. Change a life; spark a smile; make a difference; do it today!

Mistakes and Difficulties

"The person who has not struggled with difficulty after difficulty cannot know the joy of genuine success. Face the problems and fight your way over them...The rungs in the ladder of success are composed of difficulties."
-Vern McLellan

A kite rises against, not with, the wind. And just like the kite, as humans, we rise against our struggles and adversity. They are the force, the energy, that lifts us to great heights just as the wind lifts the kite to great heights. When we face our problems and fight our way over them, we aren't really fighting our way over or through the perceived problem. We are fighting to overcome our belief about the so-called problem. That which is perceived as a problem to one person can easily be seen as an opportunity to another. Our perspective determines whether a challenge is a problem or an opportunity.

If we view success as the ladder, then we can begin to understand and set our expectations to brace for the adversity we know will come as we struggle to climb. The joy that comes from achieving success comes in part from being able to look back, just like the mountaineer looks back at the speck hat represents their tent in the base camp. Overcoming the struggle that the mountain is the same as climbing the mountain of success. The joy or the climber is as much in the struggle as it is in reaching the crest or innacle of their journey.

here is something about facing our difficulties and succeeding anyway hat makes the sweet victory of success a true experience of joy. Face nd overcome your struggles, and know that both success and joy can be eached by standing on the top rung of the ladder!

Mistakes and The Lessons of Failure

"It's fine to celebrate success, but it is more important to heed the lessons of failure."
-Bill Gates

ailure is a great teacher. Don't rush past your failures in an attempt to nore quickly achieve success. Study your failure; examine your failure. here's a good chance that a clue to your future success lies hidden in he failure. With every failure, at the very least, we can learn what not to o. Failure was not an option for Thomas Edison as he discovered 10,000 ways not to make a light bulb."

Mistakes and Adversity

"Never bear more than one kind of trouble at a time. Some people bear three kinds; all they have had, all they have now, and all they expect to have."
-Edward Everett Hale

dversity has come to be not only accepted as a part of life, but also an vent to be expected at some point in time when one tries to reach a goal. Vhen dealing with adversity, should it arise in our lives, we are best served o address the actual situation that appears to be creating the adversity. Ve can only ever face what is directly in front of us, what is in the now, vhat is in the present. Oftentimes, we look to past experiences that were imilarly challenging and project the outcome of the past onto the future.

We have a tendency to bring about what we think about. If we become mired down in past difficulties and struggles, we will miss the opportunity or solution that only briefly presents itself to a clear mind. And, at the same time, it is impossible to solve a perceived problem in the future that hasn' even happened yet. More importantly, it may never happen.

If we are focused on potential difficulties in the future, then, like a magnet we can attract those challenges directly into our lives. Therefore, let us simply focus our thoughts on our desires and diligently work to bring solution only to the challenges that arise in the present and stay ever focused on the outcomes we are seeking.

If our expectation is for a positive solution, then more likely than not, if we stay focused in the present and only on what is directly in front of us in the now, we will find or create the solution we seek. Be, think, listen, and stay in the present moment. Plan and prepare proactively for the future, reflect briefly on the lessons of the past, but always stay in the present when solving challenges. Now is all there is. Challenges arise for us all and we can usually best solve them one day at a time.

Friends and Persistence

> *"There is no failure for the man who realizes his power, who never knows when he is beaten; there is no failure for the determined endeavor; the unconquerable will. There is no failure for the man who gets up every time he falls, who rebounds like a rubber ball, who persists when everyone else gives up, who pushes on when everyone else turns back."*
> *-Orison Swett Marden*

Once we finally realize that the only way to fail is to give up, then giving up is no longer an option.

An unconquerable will is the kind of will we usually only read about or watch unfold as it is played out by an actor on the big screen. As the accomplishments of someone with an indomitable will are captured for us to evaluate, we say to ourselves, I wonder what that must have been like.

We hear about fighters who get knocked down and should stay down, yet they rise again and again. The movie Rocky immortalized this concept in the minds of viewers. In real life, the mighty Mike Tyson was defeated by a "bum" who wouldn't give up.

We have countless other stories of those who refused to give up as they struggled to bring new ideas to the business world as well. Two bicycle mechanics that grew up in Ohio were also avid readers with a dream of flight. They could easily have given up on their dream, but they refused to stop trying; the rest is history.

Henry Ford had a vision for a V-8 motor that his entire team of engineers said could not be built. He never wavered from his vision even after the entire team of engineers was ready to give up. On the day the chief engineer finally came to report success with enthusiasm and excitement, exuberantly stating "we did it, we did it," Mr. Ford replied to the announcement calmly and with an even measure, "Of course you did. I always knew you would!"

Chapter 5: Inspire Others and Seek Inspiration

Learning to Steal Like an Artist

If there's something you've never done before and you want to do it, you have to learn how. One of the easiest ways to do this is to look at how those who have come before you have done it and then do what they did until you figure out your own way of doing it. One of the greatest discoveries for me while on this journey of figuring out my place in this world was discovering the work of Austin Kleon.

He helped me to understand where ideas REALLY come from. In his Steal Like an Artist, I learned "how to look at the world like an artist." In the opening of his book he says every artist gets asked the question, "Where do you get your ideas?" He says the honest artist answers, "I steal them."

Challenge Your Perception

I don't remember at exactly what age my perception of my grandpa dad changed. I know it wasn't until after I had outgrown my "anger" phase and become curious enough to consider what his life must have been like.

My grandpa dad was the survivor of not one but two major wars. He served in both World War II and Korea. More importantly, he survived endless days of brutal torture at the hands of his Japanese captors in a POW Camp in the Philippines. He rarely ever talked about the war, but one day I got him to tell me how he kept it together while being locked in the "sweat box," which was one of his captors' favorite forms of torture.

The sweat box was just big enough to hold a man and small enough that there was no way to get comfortable inside. It was a bamboo cage wrapped in tin that was designed to capture the heat from the blistering tropical sun. At night, the only light visible was whatever moonlight shone through the cracks of the bamboo.

I asked my grandpa dad how he made it through that experience. He explained how he used the sand inside his box to keep from losing his mind. I wrote this poem to honor his memory and the sacrifice he made for his country and his family. I had a completely different impression of him after he shared this with me, and I was more grateful than ever that he stood by me through my misguided angry, troubled years and my battles with my inner demons of feeling abandoned and unworthy of love and my attempts to drown those feelings with alcohol.

Grains of Sand

As early light shone through the crack,
1 grain, 2, then 3, mind now on track
Again with ritual I begin the day,
4, then 5, another night disappeared away...

Sanity, fragility, fleeting, fading,
I count the sand grains daily, waiting...
Waiting for I know not what, nor when
Hoping, praying for freedom from my pen.

Breakfast, lunch, and dinner too
One meal a day, then you're through
Seaweed wrap, rice ball inside,

Will today be the day they break my pride?

Door flung open from atop my box
Awaiting soldier his grimace stalks
Shrill command doth pierce my ears
Standing strong, I fight back fears

Questions and beatings begin again
To make you feel there's no way to win
Hopelessness is their favorite tool
I never knew a human could be so cruel

Back in the box you piece of shit
For in the darkness we wipe out wit
Terror returns as the night does too
God I hope this will soon be through.

Perception is everything! Challenge your perceptions. This lesson of perception opened my eyes to how I had once seen my grandpa dad, and it also opened my eyes about what we are humanly capable of, even if we are unsure about what we can do, be, become, or achieve.

Until the day I made my commitment to ride in the Pan-Mass Challenge, I was not a cyclist. I didn't own a road bike. I never even imagined wanting to own a road bike. I was getting old. I wasn't actually fat, but I was certainly much fatter than I wanted to be. That was my perception of reality.

So, when someone suggested to me that I could ride a bike in the Pan-Mass Challenge, I didn't see it as a possibility. It seemed ridiculous to me. Couldn't they see that I was not a cyclist? Who did they think I was to get on a bike and go do this 192-mile ride? I gave them all my reasons, all my evidence, all of which would support the position that I was not a cyclist.

They told me to commit to riding in the PMC and I would figure it out. On the day I made my commitment to ride the Pan-Mass Challenge, I opened myself up to a new perception of reality. I opened myself up to the possibility of becoming a cyclist, of becoming a bike rider.

From that point, one day at a time, my reality began to change. I became a bike owner. I still hadn't ridden a road bike, but I was now mentally prepared to become a bike rider. After I met with Terry at the bike shop, I became a bike rider -- and in time, I would become a cyclist too... I hadn't completed a single Pan-Mass Challenge yet, but "deep down" I knew I could ride a road bike.

As I began practicing and preparing myself with weekend rides, more and more possibilities opened up to me. My perception of who I was and what I was and wasn't capable of doing broadened. I saw myself differently with every ride I completed. I became more confident about the vision of myself as not only a bike rider, but a cyclist, someone who was capable of entering into and completing the Pan-Mass Challenge.

And then the day came when my vision of myself as someone who could complete the Pan-Mass Challenge was tested. I rode during the coldest, wettest Pan-Mass Challenge in the history of the event. Suddenly, that vision which had begun months before became my new reality.

If where you are right now is not where you want to be, it may be tough for you to imagine being on the other side and living in your new reality. Just your willingness to commit to that vision, even though you may not see yet how to make it a reality, is a step forward that will open you up to new perceptions of reality. You will open yourself up to the possibility of becoming whatever it is or whoever it is that you want to be.

Even once you entertain the possibility of becoming who it is or what it is you want to become, it's not a done deal until you've actually done it. However, what happens along the way is that you start compiling these small, little milestones that begin to build on each other. These are the stepping stones of possibility that begin to develop for you.

Stepping Stones of Possibility

You go out for your first ten-mile ride. After you do ten miles, you say to yourself, That wasn't so bad. I don't know why I ever thought that was a big deal to start with. And then you do fifteen, and then you do twenty. Then twenty becomes forty and then forty becomes sixty. Then one day, you go, "You know what? I wonder what it would actually take for me to ride a hundred miles today."

You know that if you ride out from your house in Henderson, Nevada, to Jean, Nevada, and back, and then do that again, you will have ridden 100 miles. You say to yourself, "Today, I'll just go out to Jean and back." And a month from now, you'll go to Jean and back twice.

A similar story of possibility comes from my friend and her husband. My friend's husband was not a walker. He hated walking. He would complain if you asked him to walk a block. Then, their family van broke down and suddenly, if he wanted to get anywhere or do anything, he had to walk. There was no other option.

At first, he struggled to walk down the block. Then, he could make it down the hill and back up. Then, he could make it to the grocery store and back – about a mile each way. Then, he could make it two miles. Then three.

Now, he enjoys walking. He routinely goes on walks that are 45 minutes each way and enjoys the time spent. It never would have happened if he hadn't lost the van.

Becoming What You Never Thought You'd Be

Irish Bob, my 81-year-old marathon-running, bike-riding friend, who had never run before and was not a runner, asked the Leukemia and Lymphoma Society what they wanted him to do for them to help repay them for all the support they'd given him during his battles with cancer. Their answer was, "You can run a marathon. You can run with Team in Training."

He started laughing. His perceived reality of himself did not include being a runner.

"What are you talking about? I can't run. I'm not a runner."

They said, "We don't care. It doesn't matter that you're not a runner. We'll teach you how to run. All you have to do is make the commitment to become a runner, and everything that you need to learn to become a runner, we'll make sure is available to you."

Irish Bob's response was, "But you guys aren't listening. You don't understand. I'm not a runner."

They looked at him and said, "Okay. Did you not just tell us that you wanted us to tell you what you could do to help repay us? We need you to be a runner."

Irish Bob said, "Okay. I don't know how I'll ever start, but okay."

They said, "You don't have to worry about that. We're going to provide somebody, and they are going to help you. They're going to reach out to you and they're going to tell you what you need to do on day one, day two, day three, day four, day five, day ten. Eventually, at some point in time, Bob, you will be a runner."

Irish Bob rolled his eyes and said, "Okay. Whatever."

Being a runner did not fit into Bob's current perceived reality. When Bob first started training, he couldn't walk from his house to the end of the block. Eventually, he was able to go from his house to the end of the block.

When he could do that, the guy who was working with him said, "Okay, Bob, now I want you to go around the block. If you can make it to the end of the block, then you can go ahead and walk around the block, and if you have to stop halfway between here and there, then stop, take a break, and then walk back around to your house."

That's how Bob started. He started walking around the block. After he'd done his first walk around the block, he was like, "This isn't so bad."

Then the guy told him, "Now I want you to run from your house to the end of your street."

Bob couldn't run from his house to the end of the street when he first started. After he was able to do that and he'd done it a few times, the trainer told him, "Bob, I want you to run around the block."

When Bob was able to run around the block, the trainer told him, "Bob, now that you've run around the block, I want you to run around the block twice."

It built from there. Baby steps... slowly, and over time, he became a runner. From running around the block, he was eventually able to run his first mile. Then, he could run two miles. Then, he could run three. Then, he did his first 5k, and it just went on from there. Then, he did a 10k, and then a half-marathon, and eventually, Bob went all the way to Dublin, Ireland, to run his first marathon.

Bob became a runner one day at a time. Bob also decided he wasn't going to wait until someday to run a Marathon. Instead, he put a stake in the ground and said, "I will do whatever it takes to prepare." And he did.

You may not be interested in running a marathon, and that's fine. However, I am sure there is something you have always thought about doing, something you would get to someday. Here is the reality: someday is never coming. It doesn't exist. It's a made-up concept for putting dreams, desires, goals, and aspirations on hold.

Go to your calendar and see if you can find "someday." It's not after Friday, and it's not between Saturday and Sunday either. It doesn't come before Monday and it's not on Humpday either. You can go through every single month and I guarantee you won't find it anywhere!

I know, I looked. It's not there, you won't even find it on February 29th. It simply doesn't exist.

The purpose of this book is actually very simple. I wrote this book to fulfill one of my someday items. I had said for many years that someday I would like to write a book. It turns out I was in pretty good company because across America and the globe it is estimated that about three fourths of the population would like to write a book someday.

The undeniable truth is that most never will for a variety of totally valid reasons. I simply decided I was going to do it no matter what and it still took me years and almost never happened. If I hadn't come to grips with my attitude about someday, I don't believe you would be reading this book now.

Becoming Someone Else's Inspiration

We often get so focused on the Big Hairy Audacious Goal (BHAG) at the end and become so overwhelmed by what that looks like and how far we feel from our goal that we allow it to stop us. I can remember when I first met Terry at the bike shop.

I watched the color drain out of his face when I told him that I was going to ride in the 192-mile Pan-Mass Challenge. He knew I'd only just gotten my bike and I didn't know the first thing about riding bikes, let alone "cycling." Then he asked me the next question, "How much time do you have to prepare for this?" When I told Terry I had about five months to get ready, the color came back into his face. He knew I was giving myself adequate time to prepare.

It's been six years since my first Pan-Mass Challenge. Now, I'm going to be one of the team leaders who will serve as an inspiration for all those other people who are signing up, going, "Okay, I guess I can do this thing."

I went from not being a bike rider and not being a cyclist to being the leader of a group of bike riders and a group of cyclists because I changed my perspective on not only what was possible, but more importantly, what was possible for me.

Whatever it is that you want to do, it's possible!

I'm six years older than I was when I first started, but I'm in the best shape of my life because I made the decision to say yes and make that commitment to becoming something I never imagined I could be.

My friend Ron, who gave me the bike I rode during my first Pan-Mass Challenge, started biking five years before his first bout with cancer because of his younger brother's inspiration. It was only because he was in such great shape that they offered him the opportunity for a stem cell transplant. He was past the age limit they normally used to screen out candidates. But because of his health level, they put him on the evaluation list anyway whereas they normally wouldn't have.

Stepping up to those challenges that we don't feel qualified to meet becomes our "yes" to something greater that's going to come in our future, something we can't even anticipate yet. We don't see it yet because it's not on the horizon for us, but it's waiting for us to say yes to the challenges that will lead us to it. This "yes" will prepare us for that greatness that's waiting up ahead.

When I committed to writing this book, I didn't have any idea how I was going to write it. I'd never written a book. I did not see myself as a writer. I'd never been a writer. I really had no idea about how I was going to write this book.

I went through the same process I went through in figuring out how I was going to do the Pan-Mass Challenge. I started off thinking about this monumental thing. I've had people say to me, "Who are you to write such a book?" They have no idea what I have access to. As Marianne Williamson put it, "Who am I not to write this book?" After all, I'm a "child of God" and aren't we all?

Sometimes in life what we need, more than almost anything, is not any additional instruction, but a gentle reminder of what we already know.

I now know I have at least ten books in me. I came to realize that if I were to write this first book, take it from start to finish, have an ISBN assigned to the book because it was actually written, and then put it out and make it available on Amazon, and eventually have the Audiobook and a paperback follow it, if I did all of those things, from that I would look back and go, "It really wasn't that big a deal. I could probably do another one of those in a few months." Once you've done it the first time, doing it the second time stops being such a big deal to you.

After I rode that first Pan-Mass Challenge in the worst weather they'd ever experienced, which was both a blessing and a curse, what everybody – literally everybody, including people who had been doing it every single year from the very beginning – told me was that if I could complete this event this one time, there was nothing the Pan-Mass Challenge could ever throw at me that I couldn't handle.

What I internally translated this to mean at the time was whatever life throws at me, I can handle. And today I can say that so far everything life has thrown at me, I have handled.

Nothing Can Stop You

In listening to all of the riders who completed the PMC right along with me say those words to me, a first timer, I realized that it wasn't just true about the Pan-Mass Challenge; it was true about life. There was nothing life could throw at me that I couldn't handle. It doesn't mean I didn't or wouldn't face the same fears that everybody else faced. I still face the same fears and insecurities, but now I have something to look back at, to reflect on, something that I've actually done and that I've accomplished. I have concrete evidence of my capability.

Brandy M. Miller, the woman who inspired and helped me to write this book, is an author of ten published books. She is just now beginning to achieve some real recognition for her work and even still, she keeps on writing. When she feels just like Kurt Vonnegut, she keeps on writing. She told me, "When I go to beat myself up because I'm not a best-selling author, and I'm not this, and I'm not that, I look at those books and I remind myself that 80-90% of Americans believe they have a book in them but fewer than 20% will ever sit down to even try and actually write it. Less than 3% will ever get it to the publication stage."

She also says: "I remind myself, famous or not, successful in the eyes of others or not, I am still in the top 3% of the world's population. Whether I ever become a best-seller or not, I have done something that less than 3% of the world's population will ever do." Just being a published author makes her a three percenter! Incidentally, since she told me those things, she has succeeded in becoming an Amazon best seller and has received two awards for her work. She has also become an international speaker.

My hope, with the writing of this book, is that I can reach everyone and help them understand that just because they've never done it doesn't mean that they can't. This book has the framework for everyone to do whatever it is that they set their mind to do.

Whatever it is that you once thought impossible, whatever it is that you've up until now said you would do someday, you will have an opportunity to do it if you engage in this process and embrace it with curiosity and without judgment.

By completing the Pan-Mass Challenge, I inspired myself to become something I didn't think I could be. By sharing my story with you, I hope to inspire you to believe you can be more than you think you are capable of being.

The Genius of Persistence

> *"There is genius in persistence. It conquers all opposers. It gives confidence. It annihilates obstacles. Everybody believes in a determined man. People know that when he undertakes a thing, the battle is half won, for his rule is to accomplish whatever he sets out to do."*
> *-Orison Swett Marden*

Throughout history, we have example after example of people who refused to quit. Did they know there was genius in their persistence? Or, did genius result from having been persistent? Did they know that persistence would eventually conquer all opposers and annihilate all obstacles? Or, did they just believe so completely, so intensely, that failure, or the act of giving up, was never even an option?

Anyone who ever makes a commitment eliminates failure from the possible list of outcomes resulting from their endeavor. They make a decision to do something and the only possible outcome available to them in their mind's eye is success because they cut off the possibility of failure with their decision.

They don't begin their endeavor hoping and wishing for an outcome. No, they begin their endeavor with the end result in mind and are committed to bringing that result into existence. The result is already real to them. They merely need to work backward from the result to discover the action steps required to support their belief.

They also have to be prepared mentally for disappointment, delays, difficulties, and discouragement.

Why do we believe in a determined person? Because we have enough history to show us beyond the shadow of a doubt, that those who believe, persist, and demonstrate patience and confidence, always, eventually accomplish what they set out to do.

The Power of a Dream

"Now, I say to you today my friends, even though we face the difficulties of today and tomorrow, I still have a dream. It is a dream deeply rooted in the American dream. I have a dream that one day this nation will rise up and live out the true meaning of its creed: -- we hold these truths to be self-evident, that all men are created equal."
-Martin Luther King Jr.

Knowing just how challenging affecting change would be, Martin Luther King Jr. rallied the people of this great nation around the cause of peace, love, and faith. A movement of civic engagement was born, and change was now inevitable despite the horrifying political rhetoric that would follow his historic speech and subsequent civic support of the majority of the American People.

Dr. Martin Luther King Jr. had a dream he shared with everyone using well-chosen words which inspired and empowered people. It was that power that resulted in his huge accomplishment. If he were here today, I believe he might ask each of us what our dreams are too. Since he is not here, I will ask the question in his honor... What is your dream? Dare to dream boldly!

Inspiration and Small Things

"If I cannot do great things, I can do small things in a great way"
-Martin Luther King Jr.

As we embrace each day for all that it has to offer, we have two choices. We can take a disciplined approach and strive to get everything we possibly can from the day, or we can just simply get through it. This one choice, this one decision is the difference between excellence and mediocrity.

In our entire lifetime, we may never be afforded the opportunity to do incredibly great things. That doesn't mean we won't have multiple opportunities to do small things in a great way and incredibly well. Our approach, our attitude, and our commitment to do the very best we are capable of, with whatever resources we have available, is what sets us apart from the average.

Being the best at something has absolutely nothing to do with being better than someone else. We can only ever be better than our previous self. The only way we can ever be better than the day before is to have the belief that we can actually improve on a daily basis. If we learn just one new thing each day, then by that very nature, we are better because we have increased our knowledge and our capacity to learn more. We get better one day at a time.

Greatness is not a position or a title. Greatness is a philosophy about being great at whatever we do. It means simply doing our best and settling for nothing but our best effort. It also means being humble enough to realize there will be days when we may not be at our best, and yet it is that simple awareness that allows the opportunity to begin again the next day with a fresh start and a fresh outlook about all that the new day has to offer. Every day commit to doing small things in a great way. Be great!

The Spark of Inspiration

"Without inspiration the best powers of the mind remain dormant, there is a fuel in us which needs to be ignited with sparks."
-Johann Gottfried Von Herder

Inspiration is a form of expanded language. With inspiration, the very best of all we are capable of as human beings may be accessed. Our minds hold tremendous potential. We have within us the capacity for greatness. Inspiration is the spark, the thought promoting piece of the puzzle, allowing us to access a higher part of our consciousness. Ideas often come from inspiration. Ideas come to life when acted upon after receiving inspiration.

Inspiration is like a catalyst in the makeup of an experiment. It is the substance required for the experiment to proceed at an increased rate as it tends to speed up the reaction of the elements. Inspiration works the same way in our minds: It gives us the ability to see more clearly that which has yet to be produced. It helps us in the visioning process of creation.

Ideas will forever remain just ideas unless acted upon with faith, conviction, determination, belief, and persistence. Inspiration is the spark which ignites our ability to access the fuel in our mind for creative effort. Once accessed, the key element is action. We must take consistent action on our inspiration so the spark can be fanned into a flame.

As the small flame of possibility grows, more and more action is added to the flame and soon we are on fire with enough passion to bring our project into reality. Our efforts literally create something from nothing, all from the spark of inspiration!

Visions, Dreams, and Champions

"Champions aren't made in the gyms. Champions are made from something they have deep inside them -- a desire, a dream, a vision."
-Muhammad Ali

Dedication and hard work are both key elements for champions. It is not the dedication and hard work in the gym or out of the gym that determines a champion's ability. No, the ability to be or become a champion begins first in the mind of the champion. Belief is more important than anything else. If the champion cannot first see themself a champion, then the chance they will ever actually become one is very limited.

Anyone can give up. Anyone can get into a slump. Anyone can make mistakes. What separates the champion is nothing we can see on the outside; what matters is what's inside. The champion possesses a winning mindset. The mindset of a champion comes from the desire, the dream, and the vision. Champions have deep inside them an unshakeable belief. It is that belief that allows them to overcome obstacles that arise; it is that belief that helps them through the pain and the struggle. What is often referred to as the heart of a champion is actually the character of a champion.

It starts with belief, a belief about what's possible. It starts with a desire, a dream, and a vision and is completed with dedication, commitment, hard work, passion, and persistence. Champions aren't made in the trenches, at gyms, or in boardrooms; they are made from that thing deep, deep, inside. Champions believe they alone define success.

Despair, Inspiration, and Hope

"Many years ago, when I was just about as complete a failure as one can become, I began to spend a good deal of time in libraries, looking for some answers. I found all the answers I needed in that golden vein of ore that every library has."
-Og Mandino

From the depths of despair and on the doorstep of suicide, hope was born. With his last thirty dollars in his pocket and a twenty-nine-dollar pistol in the window of the pawn shop, the pain of life could be over in an instant. Or, something miraculous could happen, and a different path would reveal itself. Whether we call it saving grace, cowardice, or divine intervention, Og Mandino never bought that pistol.

What happened instead, as he went from menial job to job just to survive, was he began spending time in libraries to get out of the cold. In the library, he found himself inexplicably drawn to books on success as he contemplated how he had made such a mess of his own life. Og began to question how and where he had gone wrong.

In the library, he began to study the great self-help authors of the day. He studied Dale Carnegie, Norman Vincent Peale, Maxwell Maltz, Napoleon Hill, and even Emerson. Later, as things began to slowly improve, he found the book "Success Through a Positive Mental Attitude." This book and the woman he eventually met and married changed everything.

Og Mandino attributes his success to the books he read and the changes he made in his life because of the books. The real key here lies in the words "the changes he made." Og Mandino made "massive" changes in his life. He applied the lessons he learned from the books he read. It was not what he read, but the application of what he read that changed everything. Reading is not enough; we must apply what we learn to our lives. The real key to success is read, learn, apply, repeat. Then repeat the process again and again and again until the desired results are achieved. We must learn to apply what we read to our own individual lives and circumstances. Application is key!

Inspiration and Endurance

"I know quite certainly that I myself have no special talent; curiosity, obsession and dogged endurance, combined with self-criticism have brought me to my ideas."
-Albert Einstein

There are many examples, throughout history, of people with a higher than normal aptitude in a specific area, who have accomplished amazing things.

We often assume their accomplishments are because they are naturally talented and that may be partly true. However, it is usually their commitment, determination, persistence, and hard work that has had more to do with their success than their raw talent.

Einstein believed his "curiosity, obsession, and dogged endurance" had more to do with his achievements than his talent. He also believed the only life worth living was a life of service. This may have actually been his greatest contribution to humanity.

"Only a life lived in the service to others is worth living."
-Albert Einstein

Chapter Six: Together We Accomplish More

Starting Time

It was early; it was dark. Although the sky was not yet visible, there was a heaviness in the air. Even still, there was an energy of excitement I'd never experienced before. The buzz and drone of thousands of cyclists making last minute preparations to begin their journey reminded me of the sounds and energy I experienced the first time I visited Manhattan.

Then the announcement came to please be silent for the singing of the National Anthem. It was still dark when the first drop of rain fell innocently on the back of my neck as I looked down to lock my left shoe onto the pedal.

Teamwork Allows You to Overcome the Challenges

My very first PMC was the coldest, wettest Pan-Mass Challenge in the entire history of the event. This was its the 35th year and I, along with my team, were proud to be a part of it despite the weather.

And when I say that it was wet, I don't mean just a little damp. It was wet from the very beginning in the morning throughout the entire day for 108 miles of the 192-mile ride.

In the morning, there was this mist. As we rode, initially, we were optimistic. We were all talking about how it was going to "burn off" in a little bit; then we were saying the ride was going to be cool; and we finally talked about the benefits.

"Hey, beats the sun."

As we continued, it got wetter and wetter. And then, we got wetter and wetter, and, before long, we realized that it's just the way it was. We were soaked all the way through because having a rain jacket on in that high a level of humidity just defeated the purpose. We were really better off to just be wet and let the wind blow on us and keep us at some kind of a happy medium from the energy that was being exerted during the ride.

Literally, the water was running off my face and pooling around my lips. I could hardly speak because the rain was coming down so hard it was muffling the sound of my voice. How do you get through something like that?

It takes creativity. It takes a twisted sense of humor. It takes teamwork.

When you're not prepared for it, you find ways. One of the ways we found together was humor. Humor is really powerful, almost as powerful as gratitude. After all, the reason we were riding was for those who couldn't, for those who were battling cancer, and in honor of those who were no longer with us. Yes, in tough situations, even in unexpected rain, you can be grateful!

As it was raining, and I'm not talking about a sprinkle, I had a conversation with a colleague. I look over at my buddy Mark, and I say to him, "Mark, what do you think the chances are for some rain today my friend? The weatherman said twenty or thirty percent. You think we're going to get there?"He looks over at me and stoically says, as the rain is literally pouring off his face, "I don't know, man. This is feeling about ten percent to me."

We were riding through what must have been 100% humidity. I don't know if you could have actually seen us through the wall of water that was pouring down from the skies, even if you had been there, just a few feet away.

But by making fun of that, and making light of it, you help keep your spirits from getting damp despite the cold and the wet.

That team comradery of building each other up and encouraging each other is invaluable.

"Dude, this is nothing. You've got this. I've got this."

So you ride up alongside the next guy and you say, "Hey, dude, I'd get a little closer but the water coming off your back tire is blinding."

You go around in front of them and you shoot some water onto them. You get everybody smiling and laughing. You ride on like that for what feels like eternity.

Finally, you pause and you take your lunch break and it's pouring and you're underneath the tent and you're getting a little break. "Dude, that wasn't bad. How are you doing?"

You minimize the challenges and you keep each other focused on the success that's waiting just ahead. And that's the value of a team.

The motto of the Pan-Mass Challenge is "Commit... You'll figure it out." What I realized that day was that it's really, "Commit; then figure it out." Once you commit, the universe will say, "Okay. We have a serious student here. We will now do whatever is needed to help them." Trust me, I needed a lot of help; we all did. It didn't seem like the rain was going anywhere anytime soon, so we dealt with it!

Riding through the rain like that helped to develop the framework that has become my COMMITS pathway to progress. Just like on that crazy day, it can be used to do almost anything you've never done before. It helps you take the first step so you can have the next step revealed to you in the process. The next step on that day came to us from our team leader who said, "When the going gets tough, just keep pedaling!"

Together We Can

A team is a group of people with various skills and backgrounds working together towards a common cause or vision. Our team is known as Team Flo. The Flo is short for Florence Nightingale. Our company has a long-standing commitment to the communities we serve.

Our mission is human health. We give our first thoughts to the patients and families we serve with a focus on increasing the benefits healthcare provides. Our hhc, or human health care, mission is central to everything we do as a company. Our company is a proud corporate sponsor of the PMC and I am a proud member of both the company and the team.

I would have never been able to prepare for the PMC on my own. There was just way too much to know. It was only with the help and guidance of my team that I was able to develop a nutrition and training program that would support the massive gap I had to close in a matter of months so would be ready. Nothing was left to chance.

We had a training schedule with suggested distances to ride to make sure we were developing both strength and endurance. There were short rides, long rides, sprints, back to backs, and recovery rides. There were tips on supplements, hydration, equipment, trainers, gear, and even first aid, just in case. And all of this was long before I ever had to consider how I was going to get both my bike and me from Las Vegas to Boston.

To keep everyone fired up and engaged, we were encouraged to take pictures and share details of our training rides and our progress. We had a couple of WebEx meetings, multiple conference calls, and lots and lots of text messages. I had never been involved with this type of team activity.

I found the experience incredibly rewarding. My role was to share my daily positive quote inspired messages with the team. Judging from the feedback I received, my inspirational messages were a big hit! Nancy and Lara both told me they thought I really helped to pull the team together with my inspirational messages. For most of us, training took place primarily on our own in our respective communities.

TEAM = Together Everyone Achieves More.

"Together we accomplish more" is just a different way of saying that no matter what you do if you want to be successful in life, you need to surround yourself with your own personal team, whatever that is, for whatever it is you are trying to accomplish.

If you want to be the best mom on the planet, then it would behoove you to get in connection with a bunch of other moms who at least seem to have it figured out. Now, they may not have all the answers, but, collectively, no matter what the challenge is, you can come up with an answer that fits your specific scenario.

There is no one-size-fits-all in any aspect of life. The COMMITS framework is a systematic strategy for the achievement of success; it provides a method for doing something you've never done before. It doesn't matter what it is, the process is readily applicable to almost any situation. That's the beauty of the framework or what I refer to as "the pathway to progress." And if you're wondering whether "progress" is a real goal, I can assure you it is!

Think about the way anything in this world is created. I don't care what it is, everything was created twice. First, it was created in thought, and then it was created in action. The action that comes behind the thought is what determines everything.

If you look at the New York City skyline, what you see is a vast array of buildings that became a part of the skyline over time. But before each building could ever become anything, it had to come out of the mind of the team of architects that were charged with creating the building.

For example, let's take an iconic building like the Empire State Building. Before anything was ever done, a clear set of plans were created that still exist to this day. Those plans included not only what we see above the surface but what's below the surface, too.

It's kind of like an iceberg. When you see an iceberg, you see this massive, incredible, majestic mountain of ice above the surface. What lies below the surface, which we don't see, is a quantity of ice probably two to three times the size of whatever is on the surface.

The magnificence of the iceberg couldn't be there without that foundation to support it, just as the Empire State Building couldn't stand without its foundation. Anything you decide you want to do in life can never happen without a strong foundation.

Finding the Right Team Members

You find the right team members by being willing to have a conversation with a complete stranger. There's no way to ever know who wants to, or is willing to, be part of your team. You are really only one conversation away from someone who will step up and say, "Hey, I know somebody who would really love to be involved somehow.

You're going to have some go-to people right out of the gate that you already know and then you're going to get guidance from other people along the way. I can give you a few examples of the people that were on my team. The support group where my bike came from became part of my team. The people that I worked with in the job that I did became part of my team. They were not direct supporters but they were still part of my team because they were able to think of people who might be able to help me in the sharing of my story about what I was doing, why I was doing it, and what I was trying to accomplish.

You're going to have immediate team members who support you directly and you're going to have distant team members who support you indirectly. You might even have some ancillary team members. Those are the people that you don't even think about, but who, in some way, contribute to your success. Anybody who supports your ride, your idea, or your project, is a team member.

My team first consisted of the people who "coerced" me into doing the Pan Mass challenge. I had no desire, in the beginning, to do it. Those core members of the company who knew we were aligned in terms of our values around human health care and making a difference in the lives of others were my immediate team members. The people I rode with on the weekends to prepare for the ride became a part of my team.

My team members provided the initial support I needed in terms of training, preparing to train, who to talk to, and how far to ride. They taught me to make sure I was properly hydrated and had access to the proper nutrition I needed to complete my rides. They gave me tips on fitness and stretching. They told me to get online and suggested bicycle magazines so I could start reading and learning about cycling. They were there to point me to the key resources that I needed.

There is no shortage of resources available for whatever it is that you want to do or accomplish. What you need to make your journey easier in today's world is a trusted leader, mentor, or coach to share the best curated content with you and to steer you away from the garbage. This specific team member, who is your key resource, will save you both countless hours and a ton of cash!

One of the physicians I worked with instructed me to talk with Terry at the bike shop and suggested I develop a relationship with him or someone else at the shop. They all became a part of my team.

Your team will be a combination of people who join you on purpose and by accident. Some of the best members of your team will be people I refer to as "accidental team members."

Larry McGuire talks about "The Purposeful Accident." He talks about how, once you set your mind on something, the universe will bring into your life the things you need to accomplish what's so important to you. That thing that gets you up early in the morning when other people would rather just be asleep. Wayne Dyer talks about Rumi and how "the morning breeze has secrets to share." That became part of my mantra as well. Believe it or not, that mantra about the morning breeze having secrets to share and me knowing that there's something bigger I'm supposed to do got me out of bed. Knowing there was something waiting out on the road got me up and going to get out and experience those things on the bike. It stayed with me whenever I was tempted to skip a day of riding because I wanted to sleep in.

Your team members don't have to all be people. That mantra about the morning breeze and the thought of knowing something was waiting for me became part of my team. Anything can be part of your team. Anything that helps you, drives you forward, accompanies you, mentally or physically, and keeps you headed toward your goal is part of your team.

These elements just start showing up in your life when you're willing to take that first step. The whole idea of the COMMITS framework is that everybody always thinks they have to have all this stuff figured out before they start, and it's just not possible. Parts of the puzzle won't show up until you begin. If you commit, everything else will show up for you. If you keep moving forward one baby step at a time, everything will show up for you, "one day at a time.

The Synergy of Teamwork

When I first started writing this book, I thought it had to be done a certain way. Once I got over myself and let go of my stubbornness, I realized there were a multitude of ways to accomplish my objective. Once I saw my options, I was able to choose what my next best step was. Sometimes, when you begin doing something, you think there is only one way of doing it, but as you get involved, you will discover more than one way. You just have to keep an open mind and let your options appear. Curiosity is helpful when you do something for the first time.

One place we get stuck and where we get trapped is in thinking that we don't need help or that we don't have to have a team. We think that we can do everything by ourselves. What we don't understand is that one and one isn't two; it's three.

When like-minded people come together to serve a purpose, synergy is created, and "the whole is greater than the sum of its parts." The collaboration that exists between you, your team members, and the universe creates synergy and changes everything.

Handling the Challenges of Teamwork

My team included several books, too. Yes, even a book can be part of your am! One such book titled The "I" in Team: Missing Ingredients For Team uccess, written by John J. Murphy and Michael McMillan, taught me the enefits of teamwork. In this really cool book, the authors discuss the atement "there's no 'I' in team" and their experiences with "team" as it elates to sports.

here are all these other elements that are actually the "I" in Team. One of ose, interestingly enough, is "interdependence," a concept directly relat- d to team. It's all about how we work with one another.

his book was a special source of "inspiration" for me – another "I" in team especially when I came up against challenges in teamwork. If there was omething I was struggling with or wondering about, I could go to this book nd find the "ideas" I needed – another "I" in team – to move forward.

he one principle to remember, as it relates to team, is to be prepared to and in your truth and to stand up for what you believe in while at the ime time keeping an open mind to the fact that there may be another ay or another perspective that you haven't seen yet. This is the collective ilue of the team. To be a good teammate, you need to leave your ego at le door.

here's an analogy about this old guy who is fishing. These two guys up le stream are watching him. This old guy is an excellent fly fisherman. He bringing in fish after fish, but they're watching him and what he's doing pesn't make sense. After watching him for a while, they go and talk to the d man.

Ne've just got to know something. We've been watching you, and we see hat you're doing, but it seems like the only fish you keep are the little nes. All the big ones you throw back, and almost everybody else does the xact opposite. So, could you help us understand what's going on?"

he man said, "Sure. You see all the little fish? You see them sitting over lere? You see my pan? All the little fish fit in my pan."

/e can't see everything that's true. We just can't. We only have a limited point of view. If we try to operate strictly on our own point of view we're going to miss things. We see the world through the framework of our collective experiences. Each and every experience we've had in our entire lives has something to do with the lens through which we see life. There's a Talmudic saying Anaïs Nin quoted in her writing:

"We don't see the world as it is, either. We see the world as we are."

To function well in a team, we can very simply embrace the work of Carol Dweck and the growth mindset. There are two mindsets. There's a fixed mindset, and there's a growth mindset. People with a growth mindset are open to ideas, opportunities, possibilities, and learning. People with a fixed mindset have the mentality that this is the way it's always been for them and this is the way it's always going to be. They believe this was their lot in life, their destiny.

People with a fixed mindset are like a horse with blinders. They can only see a very limited portion of the world in front of them. They are very closed-minded to possibilities. In order to see possibilities, the blinders must come off completely. Once the blinders are off, these people experience some kind of awakening. People who let go of some form of dogma, people who get clean and sober from some form of addiction, and even people who get lasik eye surgery all describe an interesting before and after, like suddenly their world expands.

That's the beauty of having other human beings in our world. We don't have to stay limited to our own point of view. We can change. But first, we have to be willing to listen, not just to respond, but to understand others' perspectives. Once we learn a new way of looking at something, once we add another's point of view to ours, we have a better view of the situation and we learn more. It's important to apply our newly acquired lessons to our life.

I didn't have any problems with the team that I assembled, but I knew whatever comes up, no matter what that challenge is, if my ego is parked at the door, it doesn't matter. Any challenge that comes up can always be solved with communication. It always helps to ask ourselves the question

What's the lesson here? If we're having conflict with another team member, instead of having judgement about the conflict, we should reflect on it, What am I supposed to be learning from this interaction that's taking place between myself and another person?

The whole purpose of having a team is collaboration, inspiration, and motivation. Without effective communication, none of these become possible. It's crucial for everyone in a team to communicate their thoughts and ideas clearly.

Teamwork and Leadership

"Leadership is not magnetic personality--that can just as well be a glib tongue. It is not making friends and influencing people --that is flattery. Leadership is lifting a person's vision to higher sights, the raising of a person's performance to a higher standard, the building of a personality beyond its normal limitations."
-Peter F. Drucker

One of the most compelling messages Peter Drucker ever provided was the message that all leadership begins with self-leadership and first managing oneself. We are who we are, we do what we do, and we become what we become, based on our ability to honestly evaluate our own areas of opportunity and our willingness to accept guidance and direction.

Leaders have the ability first to see the best in others, and then the skills to help others discover what their best actually is. They have the communication skills and vision to recognize potential and encourage an individual to raise their own level of performance to a higher standard. The building of a personality beyond either its current or normal limitations is accomplished by helping an individual or a team to see beyond their own perspective. It is the ability to see what has yet to be accomplished before it happens and providing a clear vision of how to bring the desired result into existence.

Leaders compel others to become their best. They encourage creativity and confidence. They collaborate to overcome obstacles by helping others to see limiting beliefs and assumptions. Leaders help others to interpret information in a different way. Everyone leads! Everyone contributes! We each have the capacity to lift each other up, and when we do, we are leading. Leadership is doing and being. Leadership is not just a position; it's a philosophy for success and achievement.

Teamwork and Giving

"Giving is the highest level of living; our candle loses nothing when it lights another." -Unknown

Offering a word of encouragement to someone who is struggling literally costs us nothing and would probably benefit us in some unknown or unseen way. What happens when we light the candle of another with a little bit of encouragement? At a minimum, their world becomes a little brighter. And who knows how far they may carry the flame and how many other candles might be lit in the process?

Everything we either currently are or might ever be will be determined not by circumstances, but by how we react to circumstances as they unfold before us. We were not placed on this earth to simply survive. No, we each possess within us a special gift and purpose. Our task is to become all we are capable of and to create a compelling life and to make the world a better place for this generation as well as future generations. If we pause for just a moment, we will discover our ability and potential to envision all that is possible in a world focused on the betterment of the human condition. When embracing a life of service, we will find our light has the capacity to help others to see what they otherwise would not or could not.

Our life will either be an example for others to follow or to avoid. If we are self-focused and only concerned about making a living, then that is exactly what the world will give us, a living. However, there is another choice available to all of us, and it begins with a focus on not just living, but giving. We enrich the world by walking our path and helping others to discover their path as well. Our spirit will carry us over the obstacles we face, and others will find hope for themselves as they witness our journey. Our achievements inspire others to realize that if one can do it, then others can as well.

If we fail to attempt because of fear or worry, we will find our lives more impoverished than if we had attempted and failed. Our errand is to live a life worth living. It is our own commitment which allows us to be our best and enables others to do the same. In essence, we inspire and empower others, through our actions, to take similar actions and achieve similar results. We become the mirror that allows others to see the very best in themselves and become the reflection of what the world holds in store for them.

Some things in life cannot be calculated. The history books are full of stories about people who accomplished incredible feats or came back from the direst of circumstances and almost always give credit to someone who offered encouragement at the time they most needed it. Each of us have, within ourselves, the capacity to show others things they might not see. We can help them see their path buried in darkness with the light of our encouragement.

Imagine how many other candles can be lit from just one that's willing to share its flame.

Teamwork and Service

"The best way to find yourself is to lose yourself in the service of others."
-Mahatma Gandhi

All of the great humanitarians talk about service to others. When we shift the focus from self to others, we open up the possibility to make a real difference in the life of another. It doesn't matter what our profession is, employee or entrepreneur, we all have an opportunity to make a difference.

We make a difference by rallying around or getting behind something we really believe in and then making a commitment to make a difference with our time, energy, money, talent, effort, labor, etc. We make a difference by getting involved. We make a difference by focusing on the needs of others.

One of the easiest ways to be in the service of others is to volunteer. All it takes is a willingness to make a difference and a commitment. If you have time, then give that. If you have money, then give that. If you have both, then give both. Do whatever you can with whatever you have, and don't let what you can't do get in the way of what you can.

Some are called to serve in other ways. Teachers are called to serve in the capacity of educators for our children. Some are called to serve the interests of the public good. Some are prepared to lay down their lives in the service of their country. Some are called to serve as leaders in their faith. Some are called to be healers or to work in the healing arts. Some are called to support causes, movements, or foundations. Some sing, some build, some paint, some counsel, some write.

We all have the capacity to help others. Sometimes the greatest service we can provide is to simply offer our help to ease the suffering or struggle of another. When we lose ourselves in the service of others, we find our true self.

Teamwork, Leaders, and Leadership

"Certainly, a leader needs a clear vision of the organization and where it is going, but a vision is of little value unless it is shared in a way so as to generate enthusiasm and commitment. Leadership and communication are inseparable."
-Claude Taylor

If leadership and communication are indeed inseparable, then maybe communication would be the best place to start. As a matter of record, the majority of organizations' leaders began their journey with some well-chosen words that gave meaning and clarity to the desired outcome their organization was seeking to achieve.

The best way to get people involved in a committed way is to show them how important their individual effort is to the overall mission of the company or organization. When people have a clear vision of where they fit into the plan and how their individual effort contributes to the overall mission of the team, company, or organization, they tend to be much more engaged.

Leaders share their vision about how they see the combined efforts of all of the members of the organization collectively working and accomplishing what can only be achieved through that collaborative effort. Leaders help individuals understand how they fit into the overall mission and vision. Great leaders paint such a vivid picture with both their words and their actions that there can be no doubt as to the desired outcome. Leaders generate enthusiasm through clear, concise, and compelling communication. Leaders both inspire and encourage with a well communicated vision not only about what's possible, but about what's possible when the team works together.

Teamwork and Greatness

"Man is much like a hole: the more you take away from him the bigger he gets. Greatness is always in terms of giving, not getting."
-Richard C. Halverson

I am often asked why I live my life the way I do. This quote helps answer the question. Originally, when I was creating these daily messages, I was asked why I would take the time each and every workday to create a compelling message for the consideration of others. The truth is there is no simple answer, but I can at least tell you how the process originally began. I can give you the reason I started so many years ago sharing quotes with others.

The foundation was laid in the early years of my upbringing. Raised by my depression-era grandparents, a strong work ethic was instilled, and I joined the workforce very early in life. My grandpa dad told me, "Always do more than you are paid for."

I took that message to heart. As a young paperboy selling newspapers in front of a casino in Sparks, Nevada, I often sold my allotment of papers and was then allowed to sell additional papers from the machine that stood by the side entrance to the property.

My boss, the route owner, would give me a little "bonus" for doing more than was expected of me. This reinforced my belief in grandpa dad's message. This was an incredibly powerful lesson for a nine-year-old to learn so early in life.

Fast forward to my first personal development seminar by the great Jim Rohn, and I heard the message again from him as he talked about his "Papa's" seminar in a sentence, "Always do more than you are paid for, Son." You can imagine how this affected me and I can assure you I sat up straight in my chair and took copious notes that day in the spring of 1991. Many other concepts were revealed to me that day, messages I had never heard from my own father. Messages I had never heard from anyone. Awakened now, I began the process of my own personal development.

Fast forward again to the setting of a corporate district meeting and I found my district manager at the time asking his team to make a "small change commitment" for the betterment of the team and the company as a whole.

I said, "I love quotes and find great meaning and value in them. I would be happy to offer one each day for consideration by the team." He said he loved the idea, and Kountz's Korner was born. What started out as a simple quote has evolved into the daily messages I once shared and am now once again sharing with a tremendous sense of pride and accomplishment.

I take no credit for the messages I share as they simply flow through me. At this point in time, I could no more turn off the flow of ideas that come to me regularly than you could stop the melting of the snow in the spring and the flow of water that develops from the snow as it melts.

I truly consider this a gift and am honored to have the opportunity to share the messages as they are revealed to me. This book is just such a message. I didn't actually write this book. I made myself available to receive it, and now, I have finally found the courage to share it. The more we give, the more we get. If greatness does indeed develop in terms of giving, then I intend to write until my fingers are no longer capable.

Teamwork and Kindness

"Kindness is the golden chain by which society is bound to-

gether."
-Johann Wolfgang Von Goethe

A society bound together with kindness is a society capable of accomplishing almost anything. Each and every one of us is capable of kindness. When we discover a cause we truly believe in, our belief in the cause itself will compel us to action. When people come together in support of a common cause, almost anything is possible.

"Together we are always able to accomplish what none of us could achieve alone."
-Dan Zadra

This represents the true nature of the human spirit. The human collective is a force capable of accomplishing almost anything when combined with kindness, hope, and aspiration. This collective consciousness has led to the achievement of many great advances in the world.

Kindness and togetherness linked with one another become the golden chain by which society is bound together. When a community is established based on real values, togetherness is almost a natural consequence of those values, particularly when kindness is one of the elements that makes up the formulation of the values. Together, we accomplish more.

Teamwork and Acting Together

"People acting together as a group can accomplish things which no individual acting alone could ever hope to bring about."
-Franklin D. Roosevelt

We have come to realize over the years that when a like-minded group of individuals takes action together, there is no way to know for sure just how much will be accomplished through their combined efforts. There's no limit to what can be accomplished when people come together for a unified purpose.

Winston Churchill unified an entire country with the phrase "keep calm and carry on." The phrase is almost as popular today as it was when it was first coined. During one of the darkest times in the history of the United States, a speech was delivered in Washington that would change the entire course of civil rights in America. The "I have a dream" speech by Dr. Martin Luther King Jr. unified people around the civil rights movement. With the words "we choose to go to the moon," John F. Kennedy unified a country to support the space race against Russia.

The internet has completely changed life as we know it and the creators had to overcome problems they didn't even know existed yet to make it a reality. What started as a search engine for the internet has become a company that is now leading us into the future with advances that aren't even fully understood as yet. Brands have become movements as well. The "Virgin" brand has become a group of companies focused solely on solving challenges within different sectors of society. Education as we know it is being completely redesigned by companies like "Virgin" and "MindValley."

In the pharmaceutical arena, companies are looking to understand the body at a chemical level to better understand and drive innovation. Immunotherapy was for years mostly conceptual; today, it makes up a vast part of products available to treat disease and is also key for the research being developed to eradicate not just cancer but other diseases as well. There is a short little video called "Fire with Fire by GE" that provides hope about the potential future of medicine as we know it.

Each of these causes, or major advancements in history, have one specific commonality, "togetherness." History shows us that nothing is impossible when people unite to accomplish something none of them could ever hope to accomplish alone. Like-minded individuals join each other to make a real difference in the world. Together, we accomplish more!

Teamwork and Togetherness

"There can only be one state of mind as you approach any profound test; total concentration, a spirit of togetherness, and strength."
-Pat Riley

If you belong to an organization that comes together regularly for collaboration, then you are probably very familiar with the spirit of togetherness that almost always emerges during a large gathering. When you have a bunch of like-minded individuals coming together who only meet a couple of times per year, it usually takes some kind of unifying event to help everyone see the bigger vision of the gathering.

In team sporting events, it's the job of the coach to inspire the team. He or she is charged with creating a compelling enough vision for all of the team's players to not only come together but combine their efforts for the collective overall success of the team. It is the collective effort or synergy that makes victory possible. There are usually a couple of leaders or captains that help the team see their collective potential. These informal leaders are the ones who bring to life the bigger vision the coach holds for the players, the team, and their fans.

In any team or organization, a common vision is the driving force behind the togetherness.

Teamwork and Excellence

"Teamwork is the ability to work together toward a common vision. The ability to direct individual accomplishments toward organizational objectives. It is the fuel that allows common people to attain uncommon results."
-Andrew Carnegie

For Andrew Carnegie, the common vision was not just the company, but the men who made up the workforce of the company. He knew it was his responsibility as the leader to provide the "vision" for his workers. Part of that vision had to include a better life for the workmen and their families. He knew that the interdependent and collaborative efforts of employer and employee would create success. He knew that if he could get common men to come together, they would achieve uncommon results.

"It marks a big step in your development when you come to realize that other people can help you do a better job than

> ### *you could do alone."*
> ### *-Andrew Carnegie*

In his book, The Empire of Business, Andrew Carnegie addressed the common interests between labor and capital. He believed that employer and employee were interdependent. He also believed in the advantages of mutual trust. He believed this mutual trust was accomplished by the employer helping his workmen through education, recreation, and social uplift. He also believed when the employer achieved this, he would help not only his workers but also himself.

In an effort to help build and better his team of workmen, Mr. Carnegie found a way to help workmen help themselves. He made a library available through donation to the people of Braddock, PA. He said this library would give his fellow-workmen an opportunity to make themselves more valuable to their employers and lay up intellectual capital that cannot be impaired or depreciated. The intellectual capital that a man attains is his forever. No one can ever take away from a man what is inside his head.

Teamwork and Strength

Subtle, yet strong, having the capacity for
Tenderness, and
Reflection, the ability to
Empathize, to take time to
Notice, the little things
Giving, giving of ourselves and our
Time,
Helping others.

-Bobby Kountz

Chapter Seven: Success Is the Natural Result of Commitment

Unsure To Unstoppable!

As I crossed the finish line, arms outstretched, head held high, I still had no idea what I had actually accomplished and what my experience would mean to me later. The journey changed me. I'm not talking just about completing the distance of 192 miles or that it was done in only two days. I'm talking about the commitment, the event, all of the training that went into it, all of the work, the sacrifice, the agony, and the victory, all of it. All of it was life changing.

Originally when I first wrapped my mind around actually committing to and completing the ride, I anticipated there would be a sense of exhilaration at the end. There was. But what was really exhilarating was seeing the magnitude of the task and realizing I was capable of achieving that. What I didn't know, what I didn't realize at the time, was how the event had actually already changed my life before I had ever crossed the finish line.

It wasn't until after, and only looking back, that I was able to "connect the dots." Steve Jobs gave a famous commencement address where he talked about this concept. My friend and mentor OB talks about this concept in his memoir, Shift.

What I realized after completing my ride was my life was a tapestry of all of the events I had experienced leading up to the completion of the ride. Each of the events I experienced throughout my lifetime had their instrumental place in my journey. The events of our lifetime are those that weave together the story of our life. The PMC was just part of that story. This book is just part of that story. What lies in front of me is a future I can't even possibly imagine just yet, but there is one thing for sure I now know: I am UNSTOPPABLE!

Learning From Everything

You never ever truly fail... unless you quit. Even if you do quit, that's just an opportunity to begin again with new information. The real question is if you do quit for whatever reason, is it temporary or permanent? Will your quitting stop you from achieving your goal? Have there been people that have attempted to complete the Pan-Mass Challenge or to complete a marathon who were stopped in their tracks? Possibly. Probably. Absolutely. But not all of them permanently quit. For many it was only for that moment or for that specific year. They learned in the process and took it with them to the next event and let it make them even stronger.

The Power to Define Your Own Success

"Success is the progressive realization of a worthy ideal or goal."
-Earl Nightingale

Anything you've decided to do ahead of time, on purpose, with intention, allows for you to be successful. Success doesn't happen all at once. It's a process.

As Earl Nightingale explains, a mother who chooses to stay at home with her children with the intention of being the very best mother she's capable of being is a success. The father who stays home with the children in order to be the very best father he can be and does it with intention and purpose is a success.

A person who decides, I am going to complete a marathon and completes it no matter how long it takes, even if everyone else has finished and gone home, is a success.

The same holds true for the person trying to set a record. For a runner, it could be someone like my very dear friend Irish Bob. Bob is a three-time cancer survivor who, at 79 years of age, qualified for the Boston Marathon. Even though he wasn't able to complete the event, it was a huge success. I know he trained incredibly hard and was completely prepared for almost any eventuality. Bob didn't fail because he didn't quit. Even if he had, he still wouldn't have been a failure.

How could you possibly be a failure at 79 attempting something so formidable? Just attempting it after having gone through three different bouts with cancer, being a three-time survivor, now running for the Leukemia and Lymphoma Society, making a difference in the lives of others, and inspiring thousands of other people in that process is not failure. It's success!

And just for an additional slice of inspiration, I had the good fortune of completing my very first America's Most Beautiful Bike Ride (AMBBR) Century Ride last year with Irish Bob as the Ultimate Inspiration for our "Team Carter Strong" team.

Success is subjective because it is in your power to define what it means for you, not for your friend or your spouse or your parents or your siblings or other people, but for you. You control the definition, and, therefore, you control whether or not you are a success in life. When I share this concept, it is often a game changer for those who have been wasting their time comparing themselves to others.

Empowered To Accomplish

When we control the definition of our own success, we are empowered with the understanding that, if we choose to, we can accomplish just about anything. Success is always available to us. We, as human beings, have unlimited capacity to achieve and succeed in anything we decide to.

A friend of mine walked into work one day absolutely miserable. Her bank account was in the negatives, her job was coming to an end, her rent wasn't paid, she was surrounded by people who had degrees and were making more money than she, and she felt like an utter and complete failure. She had no car, no title, no degree, no money – none of the things she'd been raised to believe were signs of success. She was working in an office where she was treated a lot like furniture – relied upon when needed and then put back where she belonged when they were done with her.

She was feeling so incredibly down on herself because she was comparing herself to other people her age who owned homes and had titles and degrees and important jobs, and here she was sitting there working as basically a glorified secretary for a group of people who didn't even really value her. All she could think was "What am I doing with my life?"

She sat down at her desk and prayed, I just need something. And then she opened up the Bible and her eyes fell on the passage where Jesus states, "Foxes have dens and birds of the sky have nests, but the Son of Man has nowhere to rest his head." In that moment, she thought to herself, would she call Jesus a failure?

Here is a man who is basically a homeless bum. He borrowed the ass he rode on into Jerusalem. He borrowed the space for his "last supper." He went from town to town basically relying on the kindness of the people that he met for food, lodging, and money. By all our societal standards – and even the standards back then – he was a bum.

He didn't have a title. He didn't have a degree. Everything about Jesus screamed, "I'm a failure!" if societal standards were used as the measuring stick of his worth. At this point in time, conceding that Jesus Christ could not be considered a failure but was, in fact, a massive success, she began to look with new eyes at what success really was.

When you follow the example of my friend, define success by who you want to be, what you want to accomplish, and why that matters to you. It's not where you live or how you live or how many cars you own or what degrees you have that matters; it's why you make the choices you make that matters. People don't buy what you do. They buy why you do it. Simon Sinek has an incredible TED Talk on this entire topic.

People buy visions. They buy visions of what they want their lives to be. This is the truth about sales that my friend would realize later. Sales is nothing more than offering to partner with someone else in helping them to achieve the vision of their dream. You ask them to buy into your vision, but only as a means of getting their vision.

It's a partnership which, if done right, creates a win-win-win for everyone involved. It's a win for you because you get the money, it's a win for them because they get the help they need in making their dream come true, and it's a win for society because society benefits from your accomplishment. The premise of the Pan-Mass Challenge, which brought an entire state and now multiple states and entire countries into the mix to get involved, is the desire to bring an end to cancer.

The vision of a world without cancer is what fuels the Pan-Mass Challenge. But if the Pan-Mass Challenge couldn't get you to buy into that vision, it would have gone nowhere. It's not the "what." It's the "why." There are very few organizations that operate the way the Pan-Mass Challenge does. Its operational costs are supported by corporate grants and things of that nature. Every rider has an obligation to raise funds to support the challenge, and every single rider-raised dollar goes directly to the cause. That's the way the founder, Billy Starr, wanted it. He knew what would happen, and that's probably why it is the largest athletic fundraiser in the country. A very clear vision and a very clear why set the tone and the definition for success.

Establishing Your Own Measures

If you're going to use this book as a tool to help you establish a business, don't use money as a measure for your success. Money's not a good motivator. The money you earn will be in direct correlation to the amount of value you bring to the customer. If you want to make more money, bring more value.

By all means, keep track of your expenses and your income. It goes without saying the basics are required to simply be in business, let alone stay in business. And yes, you should expect to make a profit; after all, that's the reason businesses are able to do all the good they do when run ethically and responsibly. Use the money you are paid as a measure for how much trust you've earned that you can and will deliver the results you promise and how good you are at actually helping your customers get the results they desire. Using money as a measure for your success is using the wrong tool. It's not the job that money was designed to do.

If you can complete any statement that begins with "I will be a success when…" or "I will be happy when…," then you will never feel like a success and you will never be happy. There will always be another benchmark you can hit. There will always be someone who has more of what you've gotten or who is better at what you do.

When you compare yourself to others, you will set yourself up for failure because there will always be someone else out there who has more, does more, or has done it bigger and better than you. Set your own metrics for success and don't define them by what other people do or have or achieve.

The one thing nobody else can do is be a better you than you can. You get to write the story of who you are and what you do with the life you've been given. You get to write the beginning, the middle, and the ending of that story by the choices you make.

> ### *"When writing the story of your life, don't let anyone else hold the pen."*
> ### *-Harley Davidson*

Just because your life hasn't gone the way you wanted it to go up until now doesn't mean anything. Each and every day, the clock starts new. A fresh page is turned, and a new chapter begins. There is no aristocracy of time. We all get the exact same amount each day. You can have a script for what success looks like today, and you can tear it up and completely rewrite that script tomorrow based upon new plans, new information, a new idea, or a different direction that you want your life to go. Whatever you decide, it's available to you.

You don't give up on the hero in the middle of a story. The hero doesn't get to claim the victory until the end of the story. We don't know the outcome until the end. As long as you are alive to continue working through the obstacles and problems you face, there is hope for you to change that outcome. If you're in the middle of the story, don't write yourself down as a failure. You're still in the middle of that story.

What happened in your past has no bearing on anything except to shape who you become by how you choose to handle it. That's it. The big difference between Hitler and Martin Luther King, Jr. isn't the crap they went through as a kid. Both of them went through a lot. Both of them were subjected to ugliness. What determined the outcome was how they chose to respond to that.

Learning to master the fact that you can control your outcome by how you choose to respond to what happens to you is a success of its own. Whether you are a success or a failure is up to you. You define success. No one else can define success for you. You have to be the one. You have to take control of the definition and it is the one thing you must take ownership of if you want to become a success.

Only we, as individuals, can identify what success looks like for us. What's interesting is you can't lie to your subconscious mind. It knows the truth about you. It knows if you have measured up to your own metric of success. It also knows if you are lying.

Noah St. John addressed this issue in his book, Afformations, in which he talks about the difference between affirmations and afformations and their respective powers. The subconscious mind can't distinguish between what's real and what's not, but it can distinguish between lies and truths as they are told by you.

I asked myself a question and tried to find the answer truthfully, *Why am I always completing each of the weekly tasks that I put in front of myself as it relates to the Pan-Mass Challenge?* My mind responded, *You know you want to complete this event. You know you want to do it in style. You know you want to raise money for cancer research and honor the people who couldn't participate in it themselves.*

Noah St. John calls that space between where you are and where you want to be the "belief gap." To get from where you are to where you want to be, you have to figure out a way to bridge your belief gap. The way we do that is by taking slow, steady, consistent actions that move you forward in the direction of whatever it is that you want to accomplish.

The way to do that is asking those empowering questions about the "why." The "why" questions we ask provide the ideas or answers to what activities we need to complete that will surely move us in the direction of what we are trying to achieve.

If you want to write the story of your own success, define what success is and write the story of how you got there. One of the books that helped me with this process was The 7 Habits of Highly Effective People by Stephen Covey, who says to begin with the end in mind. When I decided to do the Pan-Mass Challenge, I began with the end in mind.

Then, I wrote the story from there backwards through the experiences of everyone else I interacted, trained, and practiced with in the process of making it happen. Then, eventually, I started working on the details.

Once I started working on the details, they naturally came forward. The motto of the PMC is "Commit... You'll figure it out." Make a firm and resolute commitment to whatever it is you actually want to achieve or accomplish and then everything else will show up as you move in the direction of what you are trying to accomplish.

One of the challenges that came up when I was working toward my first PMC was how to get my bike from Las Vegas to Boston. That was a problem, or if I chose to look at it the right way, an opportunity. I learned, through one of my doctor friends, there are bike boxes that can be used. I had to take the bike apart and put the pieces in one of those. I was then able to keep it with me when I flew to Boston. Then I had a conversation with another friend and shared how I solved my problem. In learning how to solve my own problem, I was learning how to help other people solve their problems, too, and showing them problems are opportunities in disguise.

The universe has laws. One of them is the law of sowing and reaping, of cause and effect. When you're trying to do something to help or provide a service to someone else, there is a natural reward that comes from that action. The act of service becomes a seed planted for future success. As my mentor Jim Rohn often said to his audiences, "We're compensated fairly for the value we bring to the marketplace, whatever that is."

When we aren't being compensated for the value we bring, it's because we don't know what the value is that we bring. What we typically find is we don't know how to evaluate our own worth and how to explain it to others. Because of that, we allow other people who aren't qualified to evaluate our worth and determine our value.

When you don't know your value, it's very easy to go to a job you hate. When asked, many say they ride to that job in a box they don't want to be in, live in a box they don't want to live in, all to get poorly compensated for the work they do. And all of this is because often someone else is left to decide what your value is and how you should be compensated for that value.

If for some reason you can relate to the scenario just described, then perhaps it's time to decide what it is you really want out of life and get busy creating the value you know you are capable of creating. No one is coming to your rescue; it's up to you.

Failure Is Never Really a Failure

Failure is never really a failure until you quit trying. As long as you learn from the experience, you have gained something you can use to push you forward toward success.

One of the challenges we have is we are often looking through our mental filing cabinet for success. We pull out the file folder for our previous projects, and what we find there, instead of pictures of success, are pictures of our failed attempts, and we improperly equate those pictures with failure. They seem to have somehow taken over all the space in our folder, and we have no way to reconcile why everything in our file looks like failure.

You don't have access to anything else because that's all that's filed there. Everything you might need to believe you're a success is filed somewhere else.

Yet, if we think about it more closely, there may be something the brain is trying to tell us. It's trying to tell us our failures are successes. It's our perception of failure that determines whether those images help us or hurt us. If we see failure for what it really is -- failed attempts -- then those images we see can point to the progress we've made in achieving the success we desire. Only if we see failure as something negative do we refuse to even look at the images and find in them condemnation and disappointment.

Going back to Afformations, Noah talks about the fact that you have your CPR (current perceived reality) and your NDR (new desired reality), and in between those two points is your belief gap. All that stuff you have been rejecting or ignoring because you saw it as negative can become the stuff that helps us to fill in that belief gap if you re-examine it and look for the positives within those negatives. That is the stuff you can then use to build the bridge that gets you from CPR to NDR.

Failure is actually success in disguise because failure means you took a risk and you made the attempt to succeed, and along the way you learned something. You gained a new piece of information that will bring you a little bit closer to success the next time you try to reach for it. Failure is never really failure unless you don't apply the things you've learned and you quit trying.

Success is Enjoying The Journey

Whatever it is you want to achieve or accomplish, I can almost certainly assure you it will be a tremendous undertaking. It will require, as they say, "blood, sweat, and tears."

My friend and coach, Michael O'Brien, or OB as he is known to those of us who are a part of his peloton, has been incredibly instrumental in helping me to find my voice.

When OB finished and published his book Shift, I was ecstatic! I saw the book as a crowning achievement, the completion of his transition from the corporate world into the world of entrepreneurship and executive leadership coaching.

What I discovered, instead, was that his book was merely the foundation for all he would create in the future moving forward from where he now stood as a published author. His book provided a reference point for everything he would intentionally build moving forward.

Writing a book is a tremendous undertaking. The Pan-Mass Challenge was a tremendous undertaking. Completing the PMC in 2014 was at the time one of my greatest accomplishments. Getting through that first day was much more difficult than I could have ever imagined. It felt like Mother Nature was testing me just to make sure I was serious. When I got off my bike at the Massachusetts Maritime Academy after riding 108 miles in the rain, the wind was howling. I was freezing, I was shivering, my teeth were chattering... I literally felt like I was becoming a popsicle. As it turns out, several riders were treated for hypothermia that day. I was fortunate to quickly find my bag and get a dry jacket on to protect me from the wind. I had made it! One day down, one to go!

The second day was a completely different experience than the first day. The weather on day two was incredible. It felt like Mother Nature was rewarding us for what we had put up with the day before. I took in every moment of the ride on day two. From the challenge of an immediate climb over a massive bridge to the rolling hills, and finally to the dunes outside Provincetown, the excitement built throughout the day. I remember coming into the finish line at the Provincetown Inn thinking to myself, I'm going to raise my arms in victory as I cross the finish line, and I did! I had gone from unsure to UNSTOPPABLE!

If you do not yet feel UNSTOPPABLE, don't worry. Becoming UNSTOPPABLE takes practice. You become UNSTOPPABLE not someday, but "one day at a time."

Be patient, be persistent, be consistent. One thing I'm sure of is that even if you don't know it in this exact moment of time, you have been forever changed. I believe in you. If you do not yet completely believe in yourself, simply believe in my belief in you, and trust that you already have everything you need within you to succeed "one day at a time."

"The mind, once stretched by a new idea, never returns to its original dimensions."
-Ralph Waldo Emerson

Resources

ADLER, MORTIMER J. & VAN DOREN, CHARLES

How to Read a Book

BIVANS, STEVE

The End of Fear itself

CANFIELD & HANSEN

Chicken Soup for the Soul

CARNEGIE, ANDREW

The Empire of Business

CEASE, KYLE

I Hope I Screw This Up

CLEAR, JAMES

Atomic Habits

COVEY, STEPHEN

The 7 Habits of Highly Effective People

DUCKWORTH, ANGELA

Grit

FAISON, BARBARA

Why Struggle: Life Is Too Short to Wear Tight Shoes

FRANKL, VIKTOR E.

Man's Search For Meaning

KLEON, AUSTIN

Steal Like an Artist

LAMOTT, ANNE

Bird by Bird

MURPHY & MCMILLAN

The i in Team: Missing Ingredients for Team Success

OBRIEN, MICHAEL

My Last Bad Day Shift

OBRIEN, MICHAEL

Shift: Creating Better Tomorrows

SCOTT, SUSAN

Fierce Conversations: Achieving Success at Work & in Life, One Conversation at a Time

SINEK, SIMON

Start with Why

ST. JOHN, NOAH

Afformations

***

"When you are inspired by some great purpose, some extraordinary project, all your thoughts break their bonds: Your mind transcends limitations, your consciousness expands in every direction, and you find yourself in a new, great and wonderful world. Dormant forces, faculties and talents become alive, and you discover yourself to be a greater person by far than you ever dreamed yourself to be."
-Patanjali

Acknowledgements

In honor of my grandparents who took me in and raised me the very best they knew how, I am sure you are smiling in the glory of knowing the morals and foundation you established for me carried me over every obstacle and prepared me for the journey I have come to call my life.

First, I want to thank Brandy M. Miller because without her help, this book wouldn't exist. Brandy and I have many parallels in our story and our history. We became good friends, and she was truly excited when I told her I was going to write my story. She even offered to help, and once I realized I needed help, I let her.

We started the interview process and began a journey of what we like to call tandem writing. A two-person bicycle requires both people to do their work. The front rider does the heavy lifting, but without the person behind them contributing to the work, there's too much work to do for one person. That's called tandem riding in bicycle terminology. It works the same way with tandem writing. The person with the story does the heavy lifting, but the person partnering with them helps things stay on track and makes the journey easier. Brandy made my journey easier and she can help you as well.

Next, I must thank my dear friend Steve Bivans, author of The End of Fear Itself. Thanks for being more patient than Job. Without your inspiration, I never would have made the commitment to write this book.

Thank you, my dear friend Michael O'Brien (OB), for always being there, for writing my Foreword, and for teaching me the importance of understanding how to "have fun storming the castle."

Thank you, Jeff and Carmella, for believing in me before I was ready to believe in myself.

Thank you, my children and my grandchildren, for all the joy you bring into my life. I love you.

Thank you, Lianne, for being a wonderful mother to our children.

Thank you, Mom, for all the inspiration. I love you.

Thank you, Pops, for making the effort to help me understand what I didn't.

Thanks to my sisters and brothers and the rest of my family. I love you.

Thank you to the members of my cancer support groups over the years.

Thanks to Ron and Niani who have shown me what true courage looks like on many different occasions.

Thanks to the strong peloton that has supported me throughout my career and my life.

Thank you to the thousands of riders and volunteers of the PMC.

Thanks to the communities of Massachusetts that have come out every year to support the riders of the PMC.

Thanks to the hundreds of law enforcement officers who come out every year to support our ride by creating safe routes and controlling traffic.

Thanks to my speaking and writing groups for your support and encouragement.

Special thanks to my fly-fishing instructor and dear friend Brad Folkins for believing in me, supporting me, and giving me Bird by Bird and my "CRE-ATE" coffee cup.

Thank you, Pam Wagner, for believing in me, challenging me, and giving me unconditional love and support through the entire process of writing this book. Thanks for putting up with my need for independence and freedom. I love you.

Last but not least, I want to thank Noosha Ravaghi, my copy-editor, who encouraged me to conquer my Everest.

About the Author

Bobby Kountz is the "one day at a time" author. He believes that anything is possible, one day at a time. He's an incredibly successful, highly motivated, optimistic, multi-award winning sales professional. He declared his independence from alcohol on Independence Day. July 4th, 1990, was, as Michael O'Brien puts it, "his last bad day ever."

At the encouragement of his coach and mentor, Bobby committed to writing his first book, The Someday Solution. He's an enthusiastic, optimistic, transformational writer, speaker, and now published author. He has written hundreds of one-page inspirational pieces based on quotations on his website.

When asked what he does, Bobby replies: "I inspire people to courageously create the life of their dreams with passion, purpose, and intention, so they can make the difference they choose, live with freedom and purpose, and serve the audience they love."

Bobby has three grown children and amazing grandchildren, is a native Nevadan, and lives in Las Vegas. When not writing, Bobby can be found either on a bike, on a trail, on his Harley, or in a meeting, inspiring someone somewhere to keep reaching for the stars, not in the future, not someday, but today. Bobby believes life is full of infinite possibilities and everything is available, one day at a time.

***

If you found this book valuable and would like to experience my work at a deeper level, I would love the opportunity to go deeper with you on whatever idea, project, achievement, or accomplishment you are ready to experience not someday but today, methodically "one day at a time."

Because I still have an incredibly successful full-time career in the corporate world, I only work with a very limited number of individuals in a group setting by application only. If you're interested in taking your life to the next level, you can schedule a discovery call with my team by emailing: info@ thesomedaysolution.com If you are interested in free resources, they can be found at www.thesomedaysolution.com/resources

It's been an absolute honor to share my journey with you and to complete our journey together, please enjoy these additional resources at your convenience. Remember, "someday" is an illusion; it doesn't exist. However, everything you could ever hope to achieve or accomplish is absolutely available, and it's available "one day at a time."

In Gratitude,

Bobby Kountz, Writer, Speaker, Author of The Someday Solution

For additional resources, visit www.thesomedaysolution.com

Visit Bobby www.bobbykountz.com

For inquiries about speaking visit www.bobbykountzspeaks.com

Twitter: @bobby_kountz